My News for You

My News for You:

Irish Poetry
600-1200

edited & translated by

Geoffrey Squires

Shearsman Books

First published in the United Kingdom in 2015 by
Shearsman Books
50 Westons Hill Drive
Emersons Green
BRISTOL
BS16 7DF

Shearsman Books Ltd Registered Office
30–31 St. James Place, Mangotsfield, Bristol BS16 9JB
(this address not for correspondence)

www.shearsman.com

ISBN 978-1-84861-433-8

Contents

I. Preface

The poems translated here were, with some exceptions, written between the 7th and 12th centuries AD, making them the oldest vernacular poetry in Europe. Latin, which arrived with Christianity in the 5th century and brought a script, was the only other language in play, although there are occasional loanwords from Norse and other tongues.

Scholars can roughly assign the poems to centuries, on the basis of changes in syntax and word forms, but many that were written earlier exist only in later manuscripts. Dating is thus hazardous, nor do we usually know the author. It is likely that one was written by a druid, six by women and rather more by professional bards; the remainder are probably by clerics or scribes.

This poetry gives us a window onto a world that is in some respects very different but in others seems strangely close. There are poems about war and warriors, the geography and topography of the country, the religious life, nature and the seasons, the Viking threat, about love, exile, old age and death. They comprise a mixture of pagan and Christian in a period when the two cultures intermingled, with the latter gradually displacing the former. However, there is no simple shift or trend here, but rather a complex and emerging accumulation of pieces, as in a mosaic.

Even for people who know Modern Irish, Old and Middle Irish require specialised study and this book has been facilitated by the recent appearance of a new grammar and the placing online of the magisterial *Dictionary of the Irish Language*. In addition, almost all the early editions and translations from the great initial flowering of Celtic scholarship between about 1880 and 1920 are now available online and modern websites have brought together much of this material.

This book represents only a small proportion of extant early Irish poetry, which includes many more bardic and religious poems and longer, narrative combinations of poetry and prose, most of which have been translated elsewhere. Many of the poems here can be read straight off, referring if necessary to the Glossary of unfamiliar names and terms near the end. Readers who would like some initial sense of the background should turn first to the Contextual Notes. These are followed by Textual Notes which provide more detailed information on the sources and content of each poem. Seven originals with brief explanatory comments are appended so that readers who do not know Irish can see what they look like and understand a little of their prosody. There is a general Bibliography at the end.

Literal translations of almost all these poems are already available, although scattered across a wide variety of often arcane sources. Here, however, my over-riding aim has been to make of these originals an equivalent poetry in English, and without attempting to reproduce the very different Irish prosodies, to capture something of their form, dynamics and style. The translations are typically close without being literal, and draw on the painstaking scholarly work that has been done in the field over the last century and more. But they are offered as poetry, as texts that despite the great chasm of time, and without in any way diminishing their otherness, still somehow speak to us.

Index of Poems

Originals

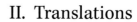

II. Translations

1

Over the sea comes Adzehead
off his head
with a hole in his cloak for his head
and a stick with a bent head

he stands in front of a table in front of his house
intoning impieties
and his followers all respond
amen   amen

2

How many Thirties in this noble island
how many half-Thirties allied to them
how many townlands side by side
how many yoke of oxen in each townland

how many townlands and Thirty-hundreds
in Ireland rich in goods and chattels
I tell you straight
I defy anyone else to work it out

and do not presume to challenge me
I who am known as Fintan the wise
the most learned man that ever was
in the whole of Scotland or Ireland

ten townlands in each Thirty-hundred
and twenty more   to be precise
and although they might seem small to us
together comprising a great country

a townland sustains three hundred cattle
with twelve ploughed fields   to be exact
four full herds can roam there without
one cow rubbing up against the next

eighteen Thirties   this is my tally
for the rich and fertile county of Meath
and one score and ten Thirties
belonging to the fair-haired men of Connaught

and fifteen thirties and another twenty
I can tell you as a matter of fact

and without fear of contradiction
in the mighty province of Ulster

eleven Thirties and another twenty
in crowded affluent Leinster
from the mouth of Inver Dublin
as far west as the pass of the drovers

ten thirties and another three score
living together in harmony
in the two illustrious provinces
of the far reaches of Munster

of the Thirty-hundreds I have reckoned
nine score altogether
and not a townland or half a townland
short in any one of them

five thousand five hundred and twenty townlands
by enumerating them and adding them up
believe me

this is how I have arrived
at the number of townlands in Ireland

3

Each one has his double   his like
though their origins differ

the O'Neills and the Scots
Saxons and Munstermen

Ulstermen and Spaniards
their ranks massing on borders

Welshmen and the men of Connaught
Leinstermen like Franks

4

I see a fine fair-haired man
who will perform great feats of weaponry
despite the many wounds on his noble flesh

with the fierce brow of a warrior
his forehead the meeting-place
of manifold victories

his eyes shine with the light of seven gems
his spear-head unsheathed
clothed in a red mantle fastened with clasps

he is good-looking
women fall for him
this handsome young man who in a fight
turns suddenly into a dragon

his prowess suggests he is
Cu Chulainn of Muirthemne
I do not know who this is but this I know
he will spill the blood of your army

four flashing swords in each hand
with which he attacks those surrounding him
each weapon used in its own particular way

and when he carries his gae bolga
as well as his sword and spear
no one can keep this man
wearing a red mantle
from the field of battle

two spears lashed
to the rim of his chariot-wheels
he transcends bravery
this is how he appears to me
but he might come in another form

he approaches the fray
and if he is not warded off
he will wreak havoc
for he will seek you out
Cu Chulainn mac Sualtaim

slaughtering dozens of you
decimating your forces
you will leave him nothing but your heads
on the battlefield

I   Feidelm   the prophetess
will not hide this from you

the blood of warriors shall flow
and it will be remembered for a long time
men's bodies cut to pieces
women weeping

all because of this Hound I see

5

I invoke the seven daughters of the sea
who spin youth's threads of longevity

may three deaths be spared me
may three lives be granted me
may seven waves of good fortune wash over me

may the spirits not harm me as I make my rounds
in my flashing breastplate
may my good name endure
may I enjoy long life   let death
not come to me until I am old

I call upon my silver champion
who has not died and will not die

may my life be as fine as white bronze
as valuable as gold
may my status be enhanced
my strength increased

may my grave lie unprepared
may death not come to me
while I am travelling
may I return home safely

the visceral snake shall not take hold of me
nor the pitiless grey worm   the mindless black beetle
no robber shall assail me   nor coven of women
nor band of armed men

may my lifespan be prolonged
by the King of the universe

I invoke the Ancient One of the seven ages
whom fairy women suckled on their flowing breasts
may my seven candles be not extinguished

I am a strong fort
an immovable rock
a precious stone
a weekly benediction

may I live a hundred times a hundred years
one succeeding another
enjoying all the blessings of life
may the grace of the Holy Spirit be upon me

Domini est salus (thrice)
Christi est Salus (thrice)
super populum tuum Domine benedictio tua

6

Like a red tide
the sons of Morna
who would be the cause of such lamentation
came south from Tuaidhe
where the waves break gently
to the white-maned shores of Cliodhna

in Dun da Bheann they killed
Maine and Dian and Deileann
three loved ones who tried to stop them
the sons of Feardhomhain   son of Feirceart

in Glen Umha they killed
Uaithne   fine son of Finnumha
and in Carn Alloidh they killed
Faolain and Follamhain

they killed the three Fionns
in their three strongholds   in a line
they killed (and this I find shocking)
graceful old Criomhall

they killed Tuathal
who was by no means a weakling
they killed Aodh and Oilill
they killed Tadhg in his own house
and the fair-haired Fionn   son of Breasail

they killed Sgiath Breac
known to everyone as the victorious
they killed proud Aonghus

and they killed my beloved foster child
lithe Leagan of Luachair

they torched Formaoil of the Fiana
taking many prisoners and hostages
they killed Raigne the fortunate
and they burned proud Aillbhe alive

in Talach Og they killed Iolann
son of Fionn and the goodly Og
Og son of Fionn
who was a prosperous man
and after whom the hill is named

Aodh grandson of Geimhnam
who now lies in his grave
Aodh grandson of Uaimidh
and Aodh of Tara (so people say)
they killed them all in Claonros

in Claonros field
which belonged to the sons of the noble Uisneach
there were many to whom they brought woe
and there Caoinche my own son
the finest warrior of them all
was parted from his weapons

after which
that little hill shall forever be called
Caoinche's precious shield

7

Hush woman   do not speak
my thoughts dwell not on you
but on the bitter clash
here at Feic

my blood-soaked body lies
down the slope near the river-bank
while my unwashed head rests here
among the fallen warriors

it is foolish to arrange a tryst
that ignores our tryst with death
I have kept our bargain at Claragh
even here in death's pallor

destined to make my sad journey
my grave was marked out at Feic
it was ordained that I should fall
to men of another clan

I am not the first to be led astray
by desire for another woman
no fault of yours   though you were the cause
how sad this our final meeting

I travelled a long way to this tryst
my comrades tried to dissuade me
had we known how it would turn out
we could easily have turned away

it was not my men who let me down
with their fine looks and grey steeds

pity that this noble forest of yews
should languish in the abode of clay

they would have avenged my death
had they lived   and had I lived
there would not have been one of them
that I did not avenge

they rode quickly into battle
keen to take on the enemy
singing in their deep voices
scions of a noble family

a strong and boisterous company
till the moment they were cut down
now the green-leaved forest receives them
a brave and fierce band...

do not linger here to face
the night filled with dread
among these who have been killed
no point in conversing with a dead man
go home and take your spoils...

sell them well   and I tell you
your children will not be sorry
or keep them as surety
and your descendants need never worry
strewn all around us here
the bloodstained spoils of war

many and dreadful the entrails
the Morrigan washes clean
coming down from her perch
from where she observed the battle

inciting us   urging us on
many the spoils she rinses
horrible her hateful cackle

tossing her hair over her back
only the braveheart does not recoil
although she draws near to us now
do not let your courage fail

I shall take my leave of humankind
and follow my youthful band
go home now   do not stay
for the night is coming to an end

people will always recall
the lament of Fothad Canainne
my speech to you will not be forgotten
if you carry out my will

and since people in future will come
to visit my burial mound
raise a fine tomb to me there
and all your labour of love
will not be a waste of time

my mutilated body leaves you now
my soul to be tortured by the Dark One
love in this world is folly
be it not for heaven's King

the blackbird with its yellow beak
conveys its glad dawn greeting
to all those who truly believe
while my words my face grow ghostly

hush woman   do not speak

8

The three sons of Ruad   blood-red kings
brave Finn   fierce Ailill   gracious Corpre

soft resting-place   their burial grounds
the darkness in which they sojourn

under Alenn   Cruachan   the bright slopes of Temair

9

I gird myself today

with God's strength to direct me
God's power to raise me up
God's wisdom to guide me
God's eye to see ahead of me
God's ear to listen for me
God's word to speak for me
God's hand to defend me
God's path to show me the way
God's shield to protect me
God's heavenly host to save me

from the devils that lie in wait
from the temptations of the flesh
from the enticements of nature
from all who wish me ill

whether I am far away or near
alone or with others

10

O king of the stars

whether my house is light or dark
whatever the time of day
it shall not be closed to anyone
lest Christ close his house on me

11

My cat and I are of one mind
he hunts mice but I too
hunt in my own way

indifferent to repute
I like nothing better
than to be seated quietly
at my books
diligently pursuing the truth
he is not put out because
he has his own small pursuits

when the two of us
are alone together in the house
each of us deploying our skills
we have great sport   endless amusement

he fixes his beady eye
on the far wall
my eyes are not so good now
but even so I focus
on the finer points of the arguments

every so often
a mouse falls into his net
as a result of his martial arts
as for me from time to time
some answer drops into mine

he is overjoyed when
with one swift movement
he traps a mouse in his claws

I am pleased when I grasp some problem
that has long eluded me

though we are like this all the time
neither of us gets in the other's way
each of us loves what he is doing
my little white cat and I

he is a past master
of the work that occupies him daily
and I too have my work to do
elucidating difficulty

12

Little strength left in my heels
tonight
I know my body to be mortal

time was I was fleet-footed
but that was a long time before
Patrick's arrival

my two legs would carry me quickly
my two eyes   burning like fires
keep watch
my two arms   exact   deadly
gave sustenance to the carrion crow
and my weapons did not lack for
the cry of victory

I used to ride swift mounts
overcoming all other champions
it was I who protected the honour of Finn
guarding his back
I was fierce   fierce when it came to it

with our swords
Oisin the son of Finn and I
dealt out our blows
simultaneously

men of great deeds   few words

13

Lord God we worship thee
maker of all things wonderful
heaven bright with angels
earth and the wave-white sea

14

Happy the reign of Cormac and Finn
alas for he who outlives them
for in Ireland then
each cow gave the full measure of her udder

alas for me who have survived
till the time after them
to describe it now
with all men robbers and the women thieves in the store

and the fish of the sea sold directly to foreigners
as soon as they have been landed
a sign of bad times

and after the gentle saints come
zealous intemperate priests
who preach strict piety
which they themselves do not adhere to

and though these worthless clerics will be bad
they will not be as bad as the High Kings
and worse still the ruthless stewards
who collect their taxes

and though bells sound in churches
and each synod is bursting with learning
chaste Christ will no more hear these
than a whisper at dawn

I am lost for words
and my eyes fill with tears
when I think that this is the sword
of the handsome Caoilte

15

Alas my hand
how much white parchment
have you traversed

the parchment will become famous
because of you
in some book

while you yourself will become
a clutch of bare bones like sticks

In this sorry world of ours
kingdoms are transient
the King who commands the angels
is the Lord of every land

even in this country of ours
where people seek only riches
there is one who preaches to us
– a thunderous message –
of God's might   his power

the citadel of Tara has fallen
with the loss of her royal sons
while great Armagh prospers
with its numerous reverent choirs

with great anguish
the pride of warlike Loeguire
has been quenched   extinguished
while the fame of Patrick's name
covers the whole land

the faith has spread and will last
until the Day of Judgement
the godless pagans have been chased
and their forts lie abandoned...

and those little cells founded
first by twos and threes
have become veritable Romes
thronging with hundreds and thousands...

the great heights of evil
have been levelled at spear-point
and the valleys raised up
exalted like hills

17

A bank of trees overlooking me
and
    how could I fail to mention this
a blackbird composing an ode for me

above my book   the lined one
here   in the glade
the chatter of birds   birdsong

a clear-voiced cuckoo in a grey mantle
sings to me
making a fine speech
from the top of a bush-fort

truly the Lord is good to me
I write well in the wood

18

If you climb up Croagh Patrick
you will see the many islands of Clew Bay

many are the feet of the flies of the world
many the treasures of Ireland
many are the stars in the sky
many the waves of the sea

but nowhere near as many
as the guests of the O'Donnell

19

Midsummer

the son of the king of Moy
came upon a girl in the green wood
she gave him blackberries from the thorn bush

and plaited with reeds
a basket of wild strawberries

20

I have three wishes
to ask of the King
when I depart this body

that I have nothing to bring to confession
that I have no enemies
and that I have no possessions

three wishes that I ask this day
of the King who commands the sun

that I have no privileges or honours
that might drag me down into torment
that I do no work here in this world
that does not find favour with Christ
that my soul is pure when he receives it

and lastly
that I be not at fault
in making these three wishes

21

Sweet bell
sounding on a windy night

I would sooner keep an appointment with it
than with some foolish woman

22

My news for you
the stag gives voice
winter snow
summer is gone

wind high and cold
the sun low
quick its course
sea running strong

deep red the bracken
its shape lost
everywhere the cry
of the wild goose

frost has hold
of the wings of birds
season of ice
these are my tidings

23

The fort over near the oakwood
first it was Bruidge's then it was Cathal's
after that it was Aed's and then Ailill's
after which it was Conaing's and then Cuiline's
and finally Maelduin's

the fort remains
the kings are all asleep in the ground

24

Sound of a blackbird
hidden
somewhere in the thicket

all is well with you

hermit without a bell but with
that sweet mild melodious song

at peace with the world

25

The cold is interminable
the weather goes from bad to worse
each glittering stream a river
a lake each crossing-place

each lake turned into an ocean
fields swollen with rain
(each tiny band a whole company)
snow-flakes the size of sheepskins
drops like the boss on a shield

a puddle as deep as a deep pit
difficult to make ones way
over the moorland
birds find no place to shelter
snow comes up to your thigh

a sudden frost makes the roads impassable
ambushing the standing-stone at Cuilt
winter has set in all over
'cold' is all people say

26

How beautiful
our peerless young king   Mael Fabaill
beloved by all
and how deserving

with his bright hand holding
the rim of his drinking-horn
and his fair hair tumbling down
over his white shoulders

I am ashamed of my thoughts
the way they stray
and I fear what this will mean for me
on judgement day

during the psalms they wander
off the straight and narrow
they run about cause trouble misbehave
in full view of the Almighty

through sociable gatherings through
groups of easy women
over forests and cities
they go faster than the wind

sometimes along beautiful paths
sometimes (I cannot dissemble)
into unseemly places

their misguided journey takes them
without a boat over the ocean
with one swift bound they leap
from earth straight to heaven

they chase foolishly here and there
and after roaming irresponsibly
all over the place
finally they come home

however much I might try
to bind or shackle them
they do not have the will

or the necessary composure
to sit still

they do not respond
to either a sharp-edged sword
or the crack of a whip
and they slip out of my hands
like an eel's tail

they will not be imprisoned
by any lock or dungeon
no fort or fastness or sea
can bar their way

O beloved chaste Christ
who sees into every eye
may the grace of the sevenfold spirit
restrain them   keep them at bay

rule my heart
O God who has created all
let you be the only object of my love
and I do your will

so that I may in time be together
with Christ and his chosen companions
who are neither wayward nor inconstant
as I am

Sad retinue
conveying Naoise to his burial mound

he whose voice
reminded one of the sound of a wave breaking

who when we were outcasts
on the run from the king's men
would cook for me things sweeter
make hazel-mead

and the two brothers beside him
Arddan with a stag or a fine pig
Aindle with a load on his back

I loved his cropped fair hair
his firm rightful desire

loved watching him get dressed
in the early morning
at the edge of the forest

my quiet warrior
whom I washed by the fire

loved those blue eyes
that melted women
and chilled his enemies

his singing in the dark woods

you think your music is beautiful
your pipers and trumpeters
but lovelier to me by far
were the voices of the three brothers

Arddan's fine baritone
Aindle's tenor
as he made his way home

you think your warriors are fine
stalking about Emain
after some expedition
but the three sons of Uisliu were nobler
as they strode back to their dwellings

it was I who took him by his two ears
and shamed him into taking me
it was I who administered that fatal draught

I do not sleep now
lying here half the night
I do not eat
have forgotten how to smile
no longer paint my finger-nails

how can I extend a welcome
to all these nobles filling the palace
who drive me crazy
when I know that the son of Indel
will not come

caught between the king and my lover's murderer
(as the king says)

like a ewe between two rams

29

My sweet pet crane
is the crowning glory of my tidy house
I could not have found a better companion
for although low-born he is a gentleman

30

If you are head of a household
be measured   calm
considerate to everyone
and make guests welcome
whatever time of the day or night
they turn up

since every guest is Christ   think of that
you should show them humility
courtesy   generosity

pay your tithes and donate the first fruits
keep to your word and forget
none of the commandments of the King

and furthermore
whatever you give in God's name
to the powerful or to the weak
be neither diffident nor boastful
for you will get your reward

and when you fast or pray
perform vigils or give alms
do not do this to impress others
but whatever you do let it be
for God's sake only

31

Ever since I have been parted
from Liadain
I swear
each day has seemed like a month
each month a year

32

To go to Rome   I declare
great labour   little reward
unless you take with you
the King that you seek there

it is sheer madness   pure folly
akin to taking leave of your senses
losing your mind

since we are destined to die in the end
to risk being spurned by Mary's son

33

I set off alone for the mountain
(O King of the sun smooth my path)
but assuredly
I shall be at no more risk of death
than if I had
three thousand men around me

though even if there were
three thousand tough young warriors
ready and able to defend me
if violent death laid claim to me
no fortress on earth could protect me

if a man is doomed he has no sanctuary
to hide in
and it follows that if he is not
no one has heard of a road where he could be slain

and even if someone   eyeing my wealth
might plot to kill me stealthily
unless it is God's will
though he might think about it
he could not carry it out

today no little person
can cut short my life
only the King who made this summer season
the Lord of heaven and earth

if someone sneezed in an assembly
it would not stop me setting out on my journey

and moving inevitably towards
that plot of ground which is marked out as my grave

it will not stop me setting out on my own

the world may have fashioned me
but it cannot dispose of me
I shall not depart this life until my luck runs out
and I am doomed
the nut does not fall until it is plucked

the brave foolhardy warrior
who at the ford
throws his pale body into the desperate fight
is no closer to death than the coward at the rear

and although it is sensible for a traveller
to take an escort on a journey
who in the scheme of things
can protect him from his destiny

for however often we cheat fate
the day of reckoning comes for everyone
with his dying breath

I place myself under the protection
of God   noble and glorious
Father of the nine orders of heavenly beings

so that even if I am on my own
He may spare me
the horror   the blanch of death

34

It is fortunate for that greybeard
in the green plains of heaven
that his grandson's grandson
became a scholar

as for me
who have no grandson nor even a son
to pray for my soul

it will be all the longer
till I meet my Maker

35

All kinds of food and drink

milk   succulent pork
the finest mead and wine
beer stronger than it is
even in Ireland

sweet streams gently
watering the ground
blackbirds' eggs a delight to the eye
the moors a purple glow

you think the plains of Ireland are beautiful
but compared to this they are bleak
desolate

and the people handsome   perfect
easy on the eye
teeth bright   eyebrows dark
cheeks ruddy as the foxglove
hair the colour of primroses
their bodies white as snow
from head to toe

a place where there is no yours or mine
where conception is without guilt or sin
where the young do not die before the old

we who are from that land
can see everyone   all around
but they cannot pick us out
shrouded as they are in the gloom of Adam's sin

fair lady will you come with me
to my shining people
for there you will have a crown of gold
placed upon your head

fair lady will you come
to that other world

starlit   magical

36

Look out northeastwards
over the great expanse of ocean
teeming with sea-life

abode of seals
playful   noble

with the tide at the full

37

It is my wish   O son of the living God
everlasting King
to have a small cabin hidden away
somewhere in the woods
for my dwelling

and beside it some shallow water
clear   reflecting the sky
a pool in which to wash away my sins
through the grace of the Holy Spirit

surrounded on every side by beautiful trees
to nurture the many-voiced birds
giving them shelter and protection

south-facing to get the warmth
with a small stream running nearby
good soil in which all kinds of plants grow well

and a few right-minded young men
(I shall tell you how many)
humble and obedient in their devotions
four threes   three fours
suitable in every respect
two sixes in church   to the north and south
half a dozen pairs in addition to me
praying continually
to He who created the radiant sun

and a beautiful little chapel
altar dressed with linen
a dwelling on earth for God from heaven

bright candles illuminating
the shining scriptures

and a building to accommodate bodily needs
eating   sleeping
rightly properly   without lust or levity
or the mind wandering towards evil

and I can tell you simply
what I would need for my existence each day
fresh-smelling leeks   hens   salmon-trout   bees
food and clothing enough   from our famed King

time and a place to pray

38

Like an acorn from an oak
he is young   yes
but has my heart

deserves a kiss

39

A large dwelling
full of people
could not be as agreeable
as my little tree-top oratory
here in Tuaim Inver
with its stars all in place
its sun and its moon

I should tell you its history
(so that you know)
it was made by the Great Artificer
and the thatched roof put on
by my beloved God in heaven

a house sheltered from the rain
safe from the threat of spear-points
and without any fence or palisade around it
as light as a garden

40

Settle in to your corner of the gaol
no feather bed for you
holy fool

alas the pack saddle of bad luck
has stuck to your back

41

The wind is cold
in the doorway of the warrior's house
beloved those warriors
who stood between us and the wind

42

Feed my son's hound
and give him a drink
and let someone else attend to Congal's hound

feed my son's hound
and give him something to drink
the hound of a man who gave food to everyone
whatever they paid

it grieves me to see Dathlenn beaten
with iron rods on her sides
I have no reason to scold her
it was not she betrayed our kin

Doilin too has served me well
she lays her head in turn
on each lap searching for the one
she will not find again...

the men the youths the horses
who flocked around my son
looked for no other protection
as long as their master lived

the men the young lads the horses
who gathered round my son
ranged unchecked over the plain
racing one another

the men the young bloods the horses
who followed my son

would pass by with triumphal cries
after some famous victory...

my son Mael Fothartaig
whose domain was the deep forest
neither a king nor a king's son
would unharness his horse there
without first looking round

a warrior among warriors
imposing his will on them all
who rode the length and breadth
of Scotland from coast to coast

the hound of the pack   he
Mael Fothartaig my son
cold now the abode
of that soaring flame-like tree

43

Who knows
whom Etan will sleep with tonight
but I know that fair-haired Etan
will not sleep alone

44

Arran   island of stags
where a whole company can feed
and blue spears turn red

crags   ridges
refuges for the nimble fawn
deer perched on pinnacles

clumps of heather
waving on the heath
ripe blackberries   sloes   blueberries
acorns on russet oaks
purple lichen on rocks

cool water in mountain streams
trout secreted under river banks

dense thorn-bushes   thickets
deer wandering in the woods

hunting-hounds   beagles
houses set back against the trees
pleasant fields
everything I tell you is true
believe me

hazel-nuts hanging from the branches
lush grass in every valley
level pastures where the swine grow fat

and the sea reaching up to its shoulders
gulls wheeling round the great cliffs
answering one another   against the sky

in any season a delightful island
and when the weather is fine
long slender craft sail by

45

Were the bright waves of the sea
made of silver
and the brown leaves gold
Finn would have given them all away

46

The bay echoes
to the torrent of Rin Da Bharc
and the waves beat down on the strand
railing at the drowning
of the warrior from Lochdachonn

a heron calls loudly
from the marshes of Drumdathren
unable to protect her brood
from the predations
of the two-coloured fox

sad the cry of the thrush in Drumkeen
and no less sad the note
of the blackbird in Letterlaig

sad the belling of the stag in Drumlesh
for dead is the hind of Drumsilen
terrible the mighty roar
of he that is left behind

I grieve at the death of the warrior
who used to lie by my side
that the scion of Dairedadis should have
a cross above his head

I grieve that Cael beside me
should have taken on the shape of death
that a wave engulfed his fair body
like his beauty engulfed my mind

sad the cry of the waves on the beach
since they drowned a fine man
I grieve that the noble Cael
ever went near them

sad the sound of the waves
breaking on the northern shore
churning about the great rocks
now that Cael is no more

sad the sound of the waves
breaking on the southern shore
my life has reached its term
and as everyone can see
my looks are gone

a rough music is made
by the heavy wave of Tulachleis
I have lost all the wealth the treasure I had
since it boasted what it had done

there is no other man I could love
now that the son of Crimthain has gone
many a chief fell by his hand
but not once even in the heat
of pitched battle
did his shield utter a sound

47

Piece after piece
woe to he who stuffs himself
the Son of God will not be pleased with him
for filling the latrine

48

O King of that glorious kingdom   wait for me
till I am pure enough to join
that final gathering
while what I have to say has yet to be heard
I envy the old   great God

Mary's son   immaculate
my Lord who reigns over heaven
prince of the bright angels
will you wait until I am old

I beseech you this with my prayer
and vow to Mary whose son you are
(if it does not displease you   O King)
that I might do something to win your favour

a young lad who is taken away
before he has finished his sport   his play
who knows what he might achieve
in his lifetime
for youth is the time of levity
and fecklessness
and we only mature with age

a calf should not be slaughtered
while it is still skittish
for everything grows stronger with time
a lamb or suckling pig should not be killed
nor a branch plucked before it yields

what sense is there
in reaping a field before harvest time

O King of the starry heavens
to pick a flower while it is only a bud
is like feasting too early

sunset in the middle of the day
morning at night   daybreak at midnight
things out of joint   wrong

I pray you listen to this plea
from my lowly unworthy heart
O Son of God
if you finish me off now
I will not profit the earth much

though even if my body
does not reach old age
I pledge my devotion O God
and even if you cut me off
without any period of grace
or time for penance
I shall not complain

for everything in the world
exists under your protection
and before I am laid in earth   O holy King
let me pray to you regularly   solemnly
as I should
to wait a little longer for me

O King of that glorious kingdom

49

Three sides I have loved
that I will not see again

the side of the fort at Tara
the side of the hill of Tailltu
the side of Aed mac Ainmirech

my husband
my king

50

Season of well-being

summer is here
branches bend under their burden
lithe and quick the roe-deer
the path of the seal is smooth

the cuckoo's sweet song is soothing
inducing an easy sleep
birds high on the tranquil hill
where the grey stags leap

heat hangs in the deers' lair
long-haired dogs lie indolent
the angry waves dispel themselves
on the smiling white strand

light breezes play in the tree-tops
of the dark oaks of Drum Daill
and galloping around in packs
the fine well-groomed horses
who in winter shelter in Cuan Caill

plants thick with foliage
the bushes clothed with leaves
summer has come   winter gone
the holly-tree pricks the hound

the blackbird who inherits the brambly wood
sings his song sturdily
in the river the speckled salmon leap
at the cliff-base the rough sea sleeps

and the sun smiles on every land
putting behind me the dross of the year
hounds bay   stags gather
ravens multiply   summer is here

Brigit   ever the best of women
golden sparkling flame
lead us to the kingdom
of that dazzling resplendent sun

may you deliver us
from the devils that crowd around us
may you triumph in the struggle
against every sickness or plague

may you free us
from the taxes of the flesh
O branch covered with blossom
mother of Jesus

beloved   pure   true
immeasurable in her honour
I shall always be safe
with my saint of Leinster

one of the two pillars
of Patrick's dominion
guarding protecting us
ever our royal queen

when we die let our bodies
be wrapped in sackcloth
and may Brigit rain down
her saving grace upon us

52

A busy yellow bee
who makes
a not insignificant journey
flying joyfully out
over the great plain
in the sun
pausing at blossom after blossom
cup after cup

and then happily back again
to rejoin
the orderly community of the hive

53

Cu Chuimne ordered his life well
(let this be his epitaph)
in his youth he read half the canon
and spent the rest of his time
chasing women

when he got too old for this
he became pious

and read the other half

54

Birds of the world
full-throated   free
extending their welcome to the sun
even in the depths of January
at any time of day
flocks calling from the dark wood

early in the excellent month of April
swallows arrive for their great assembly
leaving only the conundrum
of where they have been hiding since autumn

on the feast of St. Ruadan   an important date
it is then that they are truly liberated
from the bonds of winter
and on the seventeenth day of May
the cuckoo calls from the tangled wood

in Tallaght the birds fall silent
on the seventh of July
in memory of Maelruain who spurned
that dread omen of battle   Badh the crow
and the living pray on this day of sorrow

on the feast of Ciaran   a blacksmith's son
the wild goose comes over the cold sea
on the feast of Cyprian   a noble council
the brown stag bells on the red plain

after six thousand pure white years
when the world is free from calamity

the seas will break over every shore
as the dawn breaks   to the birds' cry

---

melodious the song that the birds sing
to the monarch of the heavenly clouds
praising his kingly radiance
listen to the distant choir of the birds

55

O God grant me
a well of tears
to atone for all my sins

I shall not conceal these from you

nothing grows
the earth is not productive
without moisture

I cannot be righteous
while I remain dry-eyed

56

Would that I were
on some island headland
on the breast of a hill
some rocky outcrop
where I could look out often
over the glittering sea

and the smooth ocean swell
the great waves rolling in
line upon line
chanting their hymn to the Father
with their eternal motion

that I might look down on
the shimmering flat strand
(which banishes dark thoughts)
and listen to the sound
of the wondrous birds
calling out joyfully

that I might hear the ripples
when they lap against the rocks
and the sound of the surf
all round the graveyard
of the little church

that I might observe the flocks of seabirds
far out over the ocean
and the great sea-creatures
marvel of marvels

that I might register
high tide and low tide
ebb and flow

that I might reveal then
my hidden name
he who turned his back on Ireland

and my heart fill with contrition
as I gaze upon all this
that I might repent my sins
difficult to number

and that I might bless the Lord
for the world is ordered
by his decree

heaven with its hosts of bright angels
the land   the shore   the sea

57

Freezing tonight on the Great Moor
the rain falls
with a dull roar
which base sound amuses
the high clear wind
shrieking above the canopy of the trees

58

Once I had golden hair
flowing locks
now all my head will yield
is this short grey crop

would that I had
hair the colour of the raven
not this pitiful lacklustre top

no longer is courting for me
for I impress no women

tonight my hair is grey
what I once was
I shall not be again

59

I have heard
that as a reward for your verse
you do not get a fine horse

but something that he can relate to
a cow

60

The flour that the mill grinds
is not oats but red wheat
the finest limbs of that noble tree
now grist to the mill of Maelodan

61

Is it time for me   O God
(whom no person understands)
after this life   which has been my right
of feather beds and music
to turn my face towards the seashore
and my back on my own homeland

to experience the hardship of battle
by the grace of our eternal King
without my horse or chariot
without gold or silver or renown

without the strong drink
that makes our kinsmen merry
my retainers   my loyal clan
without my great shield or my weapons
my goblet my drinking-horn

without the fine smooth clothing
that everyone admires
the soft cushions   no friend to piety
with only birch-twigs as my reward
and with nothing to cover my sides
but the rough skins that monks wear

and whether I should bid
a right and fitting farewell
to this great island
of the sons of the noble Mil
and submit myself freely to Christ's yoke
before crossing the Red Sea

whether I should make a full confession
quickly and sincerely
a difficult thing to do
whether I should let my tears
O King of the clouds
stream down my cheeks like rain

whether I should be prepared to suffer
all kinds of wounds to my hands
on the crest of the great waves
that can wreck a small boat
whether I should leave the track
of my two knees on the strand

whether I should take my little black currach
to breast the rolling swell
of the glorious ocean
O King of that immaculate kingdom
whether I should set out of my own free will
over the waters

whether I am strong or weak
and whether or not my exploits
are recounted after me

O Christ help me
when I take to the raging sea

62

There is one I wish I could see
could gaze upon
for whom I would give up
this golden world
all of it   all of it

even though it would be
an unequal bargain

63

My life ebbs like the tide ebbs
my skin is sallow now
the tide will enjoy fullness again
but I am filled only with sorrow

I am Bui   the old woman of Beare
each day I had fresh linen
but now I am so reduced
that I do not even possess
a change of shift

it is wealth you love now
not people
in our day it was people we loved

beloved those people
whose plains we rode across
they treated us well
without making a fuss

today you are good at making promises
then you forget
you give a little
and boast a lot

swift horses and chariots
bringing prizes to those who won
in those days there were waves of them
thanks to that generous king

desperate my body seeks out
that glorious steadfast house

where it will be welcomed readily
when the Son of God thinks it time
let him come and retrieve me

when my arms are bare now
they look all bony and thin
what art they used to possess
embracing glorious kings

when my arms are uncovered now
they look emaciated sad
I tell you I could not put them now
around some fine young lad

the young girls look forward to May-day
but all it brings me is regret
I am not only poor now
but an old biddy

I speak no honeyed words
no rams are killed for my wedding
my hair is thin and grey
thank God it is covered now

I do not mind
wearing a nun's white veil
for I had head-dress of every hue
when we sat and drank strong ale

I envy no one and nothing old
except the plains of Feimen
for while I am dressed in this drab garb
their harvests are still golden

and the stone of the Kings in Feimen
Ronan's seat at Bregun
for years storms have lashed its cheeks
but it is not old and worn

the breakers roar
whipped up by the winter gales
neither nobleman nor slave's son
will call on me at this hour

the days have gone when I used to sail
on the surface of youth's sea
the years of my beauty are gone
and my sensuality

and whatever the weather is like
I must cover my head now
even when the sun shines
my age is brought home to me

I enjoyed the summer of youth
and autumn too   but now
I enter the winter of age
which overtakes everyone

I had my fill of pleasure with kings
drinking mead and wine
now I drink whey and water
together with shrivelled old crones

may a cup of whey be my ale
and my privation be Your will
I pray O living God that my blood
may no longer boil in anger

I see the blotches of age on my cloak
but my mind deceives me
grey hairs grow on my skin
like lichen on an old tree

flood-tide
that ebbs quickly again
what flood-tide brings to you
ebb-tide takes out of your hand

flood-tide and what follows
the tide ebbing once more
I have seen them both in my time
and know them well

it is right for an island in the sea
that after each ebb there is flood again
as for me after ebb-tide
there will be no flood to come

64

A little bird pipes up
from the tip of a bright yellow bush

sending out its call
over the estuary

a blackbird on a thick yellow branch

65

These arrows that pierce sleep
at all hours of the freezing night
are the sharp pangs of loss   recalling
our love-making at the end of the day
I and the man from Roigne

unreasoning love
for somebody from another land
who surpassed his peers in everything
has robbed me of the flower of my beauty
leaving me pale and wan
and incapable of sleep

sweeter his speech than any song
save for those in adoration of the king of heaven
my golden flame   who yet did not boast
my slender soft-sided companion

when I was young I was modest
and did not go with men
but now I have come of age
and come to know uncertainty
desire leads me astray

I have all I want here with Guaire
king of his cold kingdom
but my thoughts turn
to leaving my own people
and going south to Irluachair

in the land of glorious Aidne
in the graveyard of Colman's church

to the south of Limerick
men sing of a glorious flame
whose name was Dinertech

my poor heart knows no respite
O holy Christ
from the torment of his grievous death
these are the arrows that murder sleep
throughout the freezing night

66

You raise a kitten
to keep you company
and even though you give it
all the attention that is its due
it ups and leaves you

67

These hands are wizened now
incapable of doing
what they once did

after coming to the full
the tide is ebbing now
taking my strength with it

I give thanks to my Creator
that I enjoyed life
and took full advantage of it
but the days are long now

once I was handsome
the manliest of the gathering
I took pleasure in what
women willingly gave me
but my journey from this world
is not pleasant
and my spring tide has long passed

you break up a little pile of bread
not much
for this famished wretch

one piece on a stone
one on a bone
and one on my wizened palm

68

Did you see Aed   King of Connaught
in the field

no   all we saw
was his shadow beneath his shield

69

It is time I set out my will
since for a long time now
I have been in mortal peril
my time is up tonight
in a little while
my life will draw to a close

and however difficult and distressing it is
this is something I must do
to set my affairs in order
and prepare for a violent end

my goblet of pure white silver
I bequeath to Ailbe of Emly
a fine clever and agreeable cleric
to be sent with all due haste
to the west

and as for my gilded drinking-horn
I bequeath this
(what nobler form of payment could there be
to deliver my soul from evil)
to be transported west also to Finbar of Cork
and since I am about to die
take with you as well my white silver vessel

I bequeath to Mo Chuta
my precious laver of red gold
and my staff and mitre   which I have always loved
I leave to Brenann of Ardfert
for the good of my soul

my ring my amice and my tunic
three things before which the men of Munster
would make obeisance
take them to Mainchin of Limerick
since I must relinquish them for ever

and my splendid chalice
which I have had for a long time
I hereby allocate to Senan of Scattery Island

my magnificent robes embroidered with gold
which lay once upon the altar in Rome
bear them to Lorrla of Rudana
since tomorrow I shall pass away

my blessed psalter   with the gilded edges
which glows as brightly by night as by day
and which I do not expect to get back ever
I leave here in Cashel in perpetuity

I travel in the arms of the heavenly king
setting off tomorrow across the Barrow
crossing the banks of the Suir
and on to the broad reaches of Kildare
but I will take no pleasure in this

I bid farewell to Cashel
which I shall never lay eyes on again
and to Munster   rich in salmon
since it is time for me to set off
to Leinster

I am Cormac son of Cuilennan
the service I have given
has been lawful service

I bid adieu to the world itself
taking my shroud with me

for my time has come

70

Of all the generations
that have gone before me
right back to Adam

not one remains

and as for myself   I do not even know
if tomorrow will be mine

71

May your holy angels
O Christ   son of the living God
watch over our rest our repose
our bright bed

may they reveal to us right visions
in the fastness of our sleep
O Lord of all   O great and mysterious King

may no harm or calamity
no devils nor nightmares
delay or disturb our slumber

may all our waking hours
and everything we do
be holy
and our sleep be untroubled and easy

72

A gale blowing tonight
tossing the white hair of the sea

tonight at least I need not fear
the fierce Norsemen coursing the ocean

73

My hand is weary
my pen does not produce much

its fine sharp point
slender as a bird's beak
emits a beetle-coloured stream
of bright blue ink

a powerful stream of wisdom
flowing from my neat brown hand
leaving on the page
traces of the pigment
of the green-skinned holly

I send my little dripping pen
never unyoked unharnessed
ceaselessly on its journey
creating a collection
of books of great beauty
so that the eminent people
who appreciate such things
may own them

which is why
my hand is weary

74

The days are long for one like me
without a friend except for his hound
without a servant except for his hands
without a cup except his shoe

75

Crinoc
well-measured   harmonious still your song
no longer young but still inviolate
you with whom I spent the night
sleeping peacefully
where we grew up together
in the country of the O'Neills

when first I lay beside you then
O strong wise clever woman
I was an innocent sweet boy
hardly out of my cradle
a mere stripling of just seven

later we wandered from place to place
without sinning in body or soul
and my eyes shone with love for you
like one rapt   above all evil

your counsel was always ready to hand
I followed it in everything
I loved engaging with your keen mind
rather than conversing blandly with some king

you slept with four men after me
without being any the worse for that
I know   because it is well known
you have remained inviolate

at last you have come back again
worn out but wise after your journeys

your face is darker now but still
you remain chaste at the end of your days

and my love for you is pure   true
I take you back unquestioningly
you will save me from drowning in sin
from the pains of hell
with you I will learn true piety

this changeless world is filled with your words
your path has covered every road
if I follow your teaching all my days
I shall come safely to my Lord

you bear your silent witness to
all people on this earthly sod
and every day   it is no lie
you sift our simple prayers to God

may He who judges us let me
live out my time beside you now
in peace of mind
may His countenance shine down on me
when I leave this wasting flesh behind

76

It is for this
that I love Derry

it is so tranquil
so bright   so clear   so pure

and filled with white angels
from one end to the other

77

What radiance   what blessings
to the all-knowing   thanksgiving
to the all-powerful almighty
King who rules all

glory honour and devotion
great praises pouring forth
great love in every heart for
the King of heaven and earth

Three-in-One   above all
before all things   after all
everlasting his blessing
his blessing   everlasting

78

What fools men are
to cease praising Him
when this bird does not cease

even though it has no soul
only the air

May-day   perfect day
loveliest time of year
everything looking its best
blackbirds in full voice
at the first hint of the sun

the doughty busy cuckoo
calls out a welcome to this high season
which sees an end to the terrible storms
that lacerated the branches
wreaking havoc in the wood

streams reduced to a trickle now
swift horses going down to the water's edge
the heather grows and spreads
bushes and trees flourishing
with delicate fresh foliage

the hawthorn sprouts new buds
summer smoothes the waves
lulling the ocean
blossoms covering everything

bees stagger under the burden of pollen
and the cattle make their way
up to the rich mountain pastures
to graze

the high clear waterfall
welcomes the warmth of the waiting pool
rushes stir and whisper in the breeze
raucous speech of the corncrake

the woods have their own music
which gives us perfect peace
dust gets into dwellings
haze hangs over the lake

80

A moist eye will look back
at the coast of Ireland

for never more will it gaze upon
the men and women of Ireland

81

No longer unapprised of the terrible news
the hillfort of the O'Neill

not some faint moan
breaking the silence
in some corner of the plain
but a great grief   a great noise
in every direction
a sense of desolation   loss
unutterable   unbearable

Colum is dead   lifeless
without the church that was his
how can a simple unlettered person
find words for this

God's prophet from among the elders of Sion
has passed away
no longer does he remain among us

no longer will our wise one save our souls
our guardian who protected the living
our leader who gave succour to the poor
we have no one now to speak for us to the Lord
gone is the noble one who allayed our fears

that he who spoke the truth   will not return
that never again shall we see
the master who once taught
the people of Tay

all humankind was his
all people everywhere

now the abbey is without its abbot
the harp without its tuning-key

III. Contextual Notes

Devoted readers of *Astérix the Gaul* could perhaps imagine a similar cartoon history of medieval Ireland, probably portraying the following: cattle; fighting; saints; round towers; illuminated manuscripts; and the odd Viking. The reality is of course far more complex, so much so that one risks contravening the academic law that one says a lot or says nothing. Much of what follows thus needs to be qualified and some can be disputed, but I feel it necessary for readers who may know little or nothing about the background to provide some context for the poems and offer a few leads into the extensive literature on the subject. The sections below deal respectively with the physical and human geography, language, history, society and poetry of the period.

PHYSICAL AND HUMAN GEOGRAPHY

Ireland enjoys a temperate, some might say damp, climate and there seems little evidence that it was much different in 600 AD. Atlantic storms and occasional severe winters would have affected agriculture, but the land is generally fertile, though less so in the mountainous west. There are harbours all round the rather indented coast, though fewer on the east which faces the main sources of trade (and invasion). The country would have been much more wooded than today, but there were paths and roadways across much of it, even sometimes constructed with great difficulty across bogs.

The population was probably about one-tenth of today's five million, and despite periodic plagues seems to have remained fairly stable. The people lived mainly in independent farmsteads, with some nucleated settlements, for example around monasteries; the first towns were created by the Vikings, along the east and south coasts, and served increasingly as conduits for trade with Britain and the continent. On the pattern of rural and urban settlement see Bhreathnach (2014).

The economy was based on agriculture, with the earlier emphasis on livestock becoming gradually more diversified. Cattle were so important that they constituted not only the basis of wealth but a form of tribute, a measure of legal compensation and a currency, even after the introduction of coinage. There were kilns to dry crops and water-mills to grind grain and in good times something well beyond subsistence: significantly, a famous old Irish satire, *The Vision of MacConglinne*, is about gluttony (see also No 47). Fish, which surface in a number of the poems here, were an important part of the diet (on which see Ó Cróinín, 1995) and berries are mentioned in two poems (19 and 44). Cloth production and weaving were common and embroidery was a female art. Beer and mead were produced and wine imported. The alloy bronze was made from Irish copper and tin from Cornwall. Gold but not silver was mined and precious metals feature in a number of poems (5, 35, 61, 69,) evidence probably of trade with Britain and further afield.

In school I was taught that Ireland rises round the edge like a saucer, with the plains in the middle. In fact there are few parts of the country that do not have hills of some sort, and hilltops seem to have been important in both prehistoric and historical times. In the early literature one sometimes gets the sense of a desire to map the country, to establish the lie of the land, which perhaps helps to explain the distinctive topographical emphasis of some of the poetry. Early Irish verse is often a poetry of place and the physical geography of the country – its woods, rivers, plains and mountains – forms the background to many of the poems here.

LANGUAGE

The origins of the Irish language are still a matter of lively, not to say heated, debate. Most of the issues do not have any direct bearing on these translations, but one does: word order. In poetry, word order can affect both the dynamics of the line and rhyme, and the issues are compounded when one translates from a language with one word order into one with another, as here. It is important therefore to explore this complex topic even if briefly.

Irish belongs to the Indo-European family of languages, which includes most of those spoken in Europe today. Within that, Irish is part of the Insular Celtic sub-group, together with Scots Gaelic, Welsh and Breton; there is a further sub-division between the first and second pairs. The term 'Celtic' in this sense was first used in the 17th/18th centuries to identify this linguistic cluster, and then from the 19th century as the now familiar cultural concept. Although a few Greek and Roman writers applied it to some continental peoples in ancient times, there is no record of it being used then of these islands, and interestingly a recent genetic study found little commonality in the DNA not only of the 'Celtic nations' of the UK but even within them, e.g. north and south Wales (Leslie, 2015).

While the Insular Celtic sub-group shares many cognate words and stems with other European languages (see Thurneysen, 1975) it also has some features which set it apart. While all other Indo-European languages, including the reconstructed 'proto-Celtic' have a SOV (Subject-Object-Verb) or SVO order, the Celtic languages have the verb-initial VSO, although with some variations (see Stifter, 2006: 262-64). Not only is this anomalous in European terms; such a word order is relatively rare, accounting for only 8% of world languages (Gell-Mann and Ruhlen, 2011: Table 2). (For the distribution of these go to http://wals.info/ and find map 144V.)

There are two competing kinds of explanation for the unusual word order of Irish, internal and external. The first focuses on the evolution of syntax and in particular the relationship between the 'preverb' (a kind of preverbal preposition) and the verb. The second, external hypothesis suggests that Irish may at some point have been superimposed on an earlier non-Indo-European, perhaps Afro-Asiatic language, with a VSO order. While there were datable settlements in Ireland as early as 8000 BC, a Celtic language probably arrived not much earlier than 1000 BC and quite possibly later. Scholars also disagree about the extent to which the inhabitants of the island came across Europe or up the Atlantic seaboard. The field is extremely complex and has generated a large literature (Hickey, 2002; Carnie, Harley and Cooley, 2005; Gensler, 2006; Isaac, 2007; Hewitt, 2011; Mallory, 2013; Clemens and Polinsky, 2014; Koch, 2014).

The early literature itself may or may not throw light on all this. The 11th-century pseudo-historical *Lebor Gabála Erenn* (The Book of the Takings of Ireland) describes a series of invasions culminating in the successful Sons of Mil, who are sometimes identified with the Celts and who were supposed to have come from Spain. Whatever the dubious details, the picture emerges of a layered past and thus possibly layered language as well. One approach to the issue is etymological: Mac Eoin (2007) has attempted to identify non-Celtic-looking words and names. Another approach is comparative: for example Irish and Welsh have an equative adjectival form (as big/strong as) which has no obvious parallels in Indo-European languages. The word order of Irish is also surprising in another respect. In general, inflected languages have a more flexible word order because the relationship between words is already indicated by those inflections, but Old Irish is both heavily inflected and relatively inflexible. The issues are complex, not least because word order may vary as between prose, poetic prose and verse, but readers who want to pursue them can turn to the extensive though still unresolved literature on the subject including Watkins, 1973; Stifter, 2006; McCone, 2008; Eska, 2010 and Fife, 2010.

I began by saying that the pre-history of Irish is largely irrelevant to the translations in this book. However, that misty past does present itself in some poems: in one there is a standing-stone; in another an ancient goddess; in another again a reference to the Sons of Mil; and another is supposedly composed by the immemorial poet Fintan. It is hard to tell how much this invocation of the past was real and how much backward-looking nostalgia in the newly established Christian age; which takes us on to the next stage.

Irish only acquires a developed script with the arrival of Christianity and Latin, the latter being first recorded there in 431 AD. The earlier Ogam (Modern Irish *Ogham*) line script on standing stones is mainly a record of names. Scholars disagree about the extent to which it was a native innovation or derived from Latin but it was probably invented in the 3rd or 4th century (MacEoin, 1993: 101; Stifter, 2010). It is important to remember that Latin was a foreign script, and using it to transcribe the native language must have been a gradual, complex and in some ways imperfect process (Thurneysen, 1975: 21). There may well have been written Irish texts in the 6th century, but dating is hazardous since most old texts are found only in later compilations, by which time the originals had usually become corrupted or overlaid by later forms. Thurneysen (1975: 4-12) provides a list of early sources, although his translators Binchy and Osborn point out that he should have included the early Laws among the oldest (Thurneysen, 1975: 673, n3). The earliest datable poem we have (the last one in this book) is assigned to 598 AD. As to prose, the earliest known text, the *Aipgitir Chrábaid* (Alphabet of Piety) can be dated as prior to 611 (Mac Cana, 1997: 100). The *Audacht Morainn*, a kind of mirror for princes, is usually dated around 700, and the *Cambrai Homily*, written in a mixture of Latin and Irish, dates from the late 7th or early 8th century. The first substantial written text (the *Book of Armagh*) dates from the 9th century. Datelines are disputed but the language from about 600 AD to 900 AD is known as early or Old Irish, which then evolves into early middle and Middle Irish between about 900 and 1200, beyond which we have 'classical' and early Modern Irish. The developments are gradual and complex, involving changes in the forms of verbs; a shift from 'infixed' accusative pronouns, which are built into the verb, to separate ones; and various changes in spelling, including for example *nd* to *nn* (*rind* to *rinn*, *find* to *finn*). Such changes allow specialists to date poems, including most of the ones in this book, with some degree of assurance. The nature and structure of the language is dealt with in the section on translation below.

HISTORY

History is a relative and sometimes elastic concept. To us, something written in 600 AD seems really old, but a poet writing at that time would himself have had some sense of the past stretching back into the mists of time. As noted above, the mythical history of Ireland recounted in the *Lebor Gabála Érenn* (see Carey, 2005; Mallory, 2013) describes successive invasions, notably by the Firbolgs (literally bag men) who were in turn defeated by the supernaturally-gifted People of the

Goddess Danu (popularly believed to have constructed the great Newgrange passage tomb, dated *ca.* 3200 BC) who were in turn overcome by the sons of Mil. However, we need to take the *Lebor Gabála* with a large pinch of salt: it aimed to weave Celtic elements into a plausible Christian narrative which the Irish could believe and take pride in, a kind of Celtic Old Testament. In that it succeeded and became very popular not only in its own time but long after.

We also perhaps have an unconscious tendency to compress time in the distant past, so it is important to remember that the time-span of this book is equivalent to that between 1400 and the present. The period 600-1200 saw much less change than the modern one but the history can be seen in terms of a number of interlinked narratives which played out during those centuries. Each of these is complex in itself, but it may be useful to flag them up here, so that references and allusions in the poetry can be seen in context. Readers who want to explore the period in more depth can turn to Ó Cróinín (1995) or the first volume of the more comprehensive *Oxford History of Ireland*.

The first narrative is that of Christian *conversion*: the gradual spread and in due course domination of the 'new' religion. Many of the poems in this book relate to this; for a detailed account and discussion of the many issues see Charles-Edwards (2000). After the initial work of Palladius and St. Patrick, the first probably in Leinster and the second further north, in the middle of the fifth century, an important marker at the beginning of our period is the death of the exiled St. Columba/Columcille in 597, by which time Christian influence was widespread if still not hegemonic. Although St. Patrick had attempted to establish a diocesan structure on the Roman model, early Irish Christianity was primarily centred around monasteries, with one of the most important, Clonmacnoise, being founded in 546. Many others followed. Armagh became established as the centre of the Irish church, although some of the large and powerful monasteries were relatively independent. By 800, some people felt the need to reinvigorate the faith with a new ascetic movement, the *Céli Dé* (Servants or Companions of God). Over time, and through synods and other councils, differences that had grown up between Christian practice in Ireland and the rest of Europe, for example in regard to the tonsure, penance and the date of Easter, were gradually resolved, and after the Fourth Lateran Council in 1215, Christianity in Ireland was wholly dominant and orthodox in Roman Catholic terms, although as some poems demonstrate this did not preclude literary nostalgia for an idealised, heroic pre-Christian past.

The second narrative is that of *internal politics*. Political structures and allegiances in Ireland were typically local (witness the large number of tribal 'kings'). Such local groupings would form temporary alliances, which sometimes came together at regional or provincial level, which in turn sometimes competed for national supremacy. However the 'high king' (*ard rí*) was by no means always as powerful as the title suggests, and the whole picture remained patchy and shifting. Some of the poems in this book relate to local or regional conflicts (4, 6, 8, 12,) although it is often difficult to disentangle history from myth. The literary roll-call of heroes and battles can give the impression that the country was in a state of chronic turmoil throughout the period, but peace and prosperity can seem boring to poets and we need to allow for that.

A third narrative is the *Viking* one. The first Viking raid occurred in 795, and the subsequent story of rape and pillage is well known (see the famous little poem No 72). The Vikings came in various waves, and used the rivers to penetrate well inland, striking without warning. Less well-known is the fact that the Vikings also settled and traded, establishing coastal towns, including Dublin, some of which betray their origins (Wexf(j)ord, Waterf(j)ord) and that even after the watershed Battle of Clontarf in 1014, many remained, intermarried and became assimilated. There is a fourth narrative, that of the *Normans*, but this does not intrude on any of the poems here. There are references to Saxons (which would have meant English) and Franks (continental Europeans) in one poem (3) but the long story of the Norman and English conquest of Ireland would come later. In fact, the first wave of Normans went native, intermarried and became an integral part of the existing Gaelic culture, which saw a major revival in the 14th century.

The nature and structure of medieval Irish society have been comprehensively explored in a number of books, including Charles-Edwards (2000), Richter (2005) and Bhreathnach (2014). The social, political and religious characteristics of the society were complex and interwoven, and only a few broad points can be made here. The 600-year timespan must make us cautious about generalisation, but in some respects the social structures and culture seem to have remained relatively stable over time, a point emphasised by Richter. Although MacNiocaill (1968-71) refers to a 13th century legal source, his account probably holds broadly true for earlier centuries. The picture he paints is of a highly stratified society; Richter (2005: 17) provides a useful diagram. The main divisions were between nobles, commoners and slaves, with various gradations within these classes. Slaves, both men and women, were acquired either through internal conquest or raids on Britain and only rarely became free. Some commoners were independent but most were client-farmers for local nobles, the relationship being based not on land as in other feudal systems but cattle (Charles-Edwards, 2000: 71-80). The various grades of nobles owed allegiance and tribute to the tribal king, of whom there were probably about 150. There was some social mobility, both up and down, but this would normally take several generations to be formalised.

Although it was thus a hierarchical society, there were multiple hierarchies. Alongside the main social hierarchy there was the ecclesiastical hierarchy and the hierarchy of the learned class, the *áes dána*, the poets and scholars. In the case of king-bishops, the first two merged (see No 69) and Bhreathnach (2014) has an interesting chapter on the sacred aspects of kingship in both pagan and Christian times. As Charles-Edwards (2006: 124-136) points out, the relative status of the three hierarchies was to some extent incommensurable, but the plurality of status and power meant that early Irish society was more complex and less rigid than it might otherwise have been.

Such differences in status were defined partly by the types of civil compensation people could expect if they were wronged in some way, and this points to a second feature of the society: the existence of developed legal codes. Early Ireland had a largely independent judiciary, although Bitel (1996: 20) notes that 'Early Irish laws were jurists' notebooks rather than enacted legislation'. Law-making was originally in the hands of the poets, and although we now think of law and literature as quite separate, they were close then and the former drew on the latter for exemplary cases (Stacey, 2005). However over time the law was wrested from the poets by lawyers on the grounds that they spoke in 'dark language' (some people might think lawyers are not much better). Broadly speaking, the native Brehon laws emphasised compensation rather than punishment; for example a person who wounded someone was required to maintain him until he regained health. There was some conflict between existing native laws, which allowed for both polygamy and divorce, and Christian canon law, but in general the two codes seem to have co-existed without too much friction. Early Irish law is an academic specialism in its own right, an indication of its complexity: for an overview see the chapter on 'Law, family and community' in Ó Cróinín (1995: 110-46) who notes among other things that the old legal texts were probably more schematic than actual practice. See also the chapter on 'Early Irish Literature and Law' in Ó Cathasaigh (2014).

The sense of (extended) family, kinship and community was strong and provided the basic structure of the society, the glue that held it together (Charles-Edwards, 2000: 80-123). Kinship and relationships were also underpinned by detailed legal prescription, even addressing such rights as privacy. However, social norms among the nobles were also reinforced by the power of poets publicly to praise or blame. The function of poets was partly a memorial one, to hold in trust the collective recollection of past events, mythical or real, to recount and celebrate genealogy and to legitimate and praise the current rulers; conversely, their satire was feared and could lead to ill-health and even (reputedly) death. (For a general study of the latter, including translations of 86 satirical poems, see McLaughlin, 2008. Many of the poems are sheer, if highly imaginative, invective rather than satire.) Poets were expected to have qualities ranging from the technical to the magical (Nagy, 1981; Carey, 1997). The professional training of bards was arduous, but it is worth pointing out that most of the poems here were not written by them. This suggests that the feel for poetry and grasp of its techniques must have been quite widespread, especially among the religious orders.

The first full-length book on women in this age was Bitel (1996). Since then feminist scholarship has explored various aspects of the field and there is now a substantial literature, some of it challenging earlier male-generated stereotypes (see for example Sheehan and Dooley, 2013). Bitel distinguishes sharply between the depiction of women by the 'literati', sometimes as warriors, sorceresses or mythical beings, and their actual, everyday lives. In society, women had a secondary status, confined mainly to their familial roles, although within these they seem to have been relatively secure and had considerable legal protection (Bitel, 1996: 111-137). Some poems refer to easy or tempting women (21, 27, 43, 53,); there were prostitutes in and around the courts, kings and heroes had their pick of female admirers, and monks often saw women as a threat to their virtue. Some of the poems in this collection are probably by women (26, 28, 38, 62, 63, 65). Fostering was common and created inter-familial bonds. However, children would have been regarded as adults at a much earlier age than now. For a detailed discussion of family structures, the role of women and the practice of fostering see Bhreathnach (2014).

One further point about gender should be made. Although Celtic society was largely male-dominated, paradoxically the feminine element played an important part in Celtic cosmology, both beneficent and maleficent, in the form of goddesses and other manifestations. These largely predate our period, although they feature in three poems, Nos 5, 7 and 35. See for example the entries on 'Bodb', 'Morrigan' and 'Tuatha De' in Koch and Minard (2012).

As regards leisure pursuits, music is referred to in a range of poems and played an important part in both the social and religious life of the country. Hunting with hounds was a favourite pastime of warriors and nobles, and there are references in other texts to board-games such as *fidchell* which is sometimes compared to chess. The recitation of poetry and telling of stories was an important part of court life. Social structures and norms are explicit in some poems but implicit in many more, including one about a pet crane (29) and another about bees (52).

POETRY

The classification of early Irish poetry is simpler than that of the language, and the phrase commonly covers work from about 600 AD to 1200 AD; 'about' because we often cannot be quite sure when something was written. The term medieval is also frequently used, although 'medieval' belongs to a continental European historical schema of classical, medieval (*media aevum* = middle age) and modern, which does not quite fit the Irish case, given the absence of the first.

There are three main sources of early Irish poetry. The earliest, dating from the 7th to 9th centuries, comprises mainly short poems written in the margins of religious or grammatical texts. The latter were written or transcribed by monks and some of them have been found outside Ireland, in European countries where the clerics had gone as missionaries. One can imagine that these monks, perhaps fed up or homesick, suddenly felt the urge to give expression to their memories or feelings, and these little verses remain among the most touching and accessible of anything from the period. One poem in this book was probably penned by someone transcribing a Latin grammar, a common but necessary chore; another was found in a monastery in Austria. One caution about these marginalia relates to form: the poems had to be squeezed into small spaces, and that may have affected their lay-out. Modern editions often set them out differently, and with modern punctuation.

The second main source for the poetry of the period is the various early Irish 'books' which have come down to us, somewhat imperfectly, in manuscript form. I have already mentioned the earliest of these, the 9th century *Book of Armagh*, although it consists of prose texts connected with St. Patrick, not poetry. However, the 10th/11th century Book of Hymns (*Liber Hymnorum*) the 12th century Book of the Dun Cow (*Lebor na hUidre*) and above all what has come to be known as the *Book of Leinster* (also 12th century) contain mixtures of prose and poetry which are a veritable treasure-trove. The last in particular is a rich source, although some pages became detached over time. These books often contain poetry composed well before their compilation, and scholars sometimes need to turn archaeologist in unearthing Early Irish linguistic forms which have become overlaid or obscured by Middle Irish ones. Conversely, later poets or scribes sometimes deliberately used archaic forms to give their work a veneer of antiquity.

The later the compilation the more difficult the problem of dating and it is generally most acute in the third main source: books or other documents written after 1200. Among these should be mentioned the *Book of Lecan* and *Yellow Book of Lecan*, and the *Book of Ballymote*, both 14th century, the Speckled Book (*Leabhar Breac*) so called because of its cover, in the 15th century, and the *Annals of the Four Masters* and the *Duanaire Finn* (the Poems of/about Finn) both 17th century. Most of the poems in that book are clearly more modern, but several appear to go back in some form to the *Book of Leinster*. That said, we need to be aware of Colm Ó Lochlainn's general warning about dating: 'The plain truth is that at least 80 per cent of the poetry said to belong to the pre-Norman period really dates from the time of the great Irish rally in the mid-fourteenth century, when the pride of the victorious local chiefs was being puffed up by a host of poets who, being also chroniclers, strove to substantiate extravagant claims by invoking the names of bygone scholars and sages, and by stuffing the books of history, genealogy and even topography with poems ascribed to phantom poets of the past'. He goes on to argue that had Kuno Meyer, one of the best-known modern scholars, lived longer, he might well have reviewed the authenticity of some of his earlier editions and translations (Ó Lochlainn, 1943). As against this Carney writes: 'A study of certain metrical problems has convinced me in recent times that a not inconsiderable amount of early Irish verse can be dated to *ca.* 500, a dating that Murphy, amongst others, would have regarded as inconceivable' (Carney, 1970). In a later article, he proposes a detailed, chronological list of poems dated 500-1090: see Carney (1983). Murray (2012) after reviewing 59 poems in the Finn cycle, concludes by doubting whether it will ever be possible to date them precisely. Such dating is clearly intrinsic to scholarship, though perhaps somewhat less important to the general reader, and one has to ask: what difference does it make in any given case to the actual reading of the text? I have done what I can to indicate the most likely provenance of each poem but in many cases it remains uncertain.

The history of the various manuscript sources is complex and often accident-ridden. Pages became detached or added, copies were sometimes made, often with textual variants, revised spelling or simple mistakes, and the manuscripts themselves passed from one owner or institution to another. Some have clearly been lost; others have turned up in unlikely places. The main repositories are now the major libraries and universities in Ireland, England and continental Europe, together with some religious institutions. Some scholars and clerics in the 18th and 19th centuries were aware of their existence, but it was not until about 1880 that this literature began really to be rediscovered. The decades between 1880 and 1920 saw a remarkable, international flowering of Celtic scholarship, which led to the first printed editions of many manuscripts or texts, and the creation of several key scholarly journals.

Much of this early scholarship focused on the language itself, hardly surprising since so little about it had been documented up to that point. One can still sense the excitement of the early scholars at what they were discovering or re-discovering, an enthusiasm which also nurtured the more general Gaelic cultural revival and the project of attaining national self-determination and independence. This period also saw the first translations of many early Irish texts, including poems, into English or German.

The first generation of scholars in the field were often preoccupied with the form and prosody of the poetry they were editing and translating, to an extent that can now seem obsessive. However, there were reasons for this. The academic study of modern literatures was relatively new, and although early Irish was clearly not modern, it was still 'new' in scholarly terms. The high status of the classics, Greek and Latin, loomed over all such *arriviste* endeavours, and classical studies of course involve a major linguistic element. Such a model led to a heavily philological emphasis in the study of modern literatures, to stiffen it and provide some 'backbone': witness, for example, the inclusion of Anglo-Saxon in the Oxford English degree. Secondly, Celtic scholars were well aware that, in true colonial fashion, some English and other scholars looked down on Irish as a 'primitive' language and culture; witness the defensive preface to Kuno Meyer's *Ancient Irish Poetry*, first published in 1913. Thirdly, however, scholars must also have gradually become aware that this early poetry, far from being metrically or formally simple, was in fact highly refined.

A debate has also gone on for some time about the impact of Latin poetry and poetics on early Irish verse. This is part of a more general 'nativist/non-nativist' controversy (Wooding, 2009). 'Nativists' focussed on what was indigenous in early Irish literature, in terms of the language, pagan religion and heroic or pre-historical references. The anti-nativist reaction (see Carney, 1955) in contrast focussed on what was European, Christian and Latin. The nativist reading can be seen as part of the task of excavating a historically distinct and authentic culture which could underpin the broader project of nation-building. However, the arrival of Latin with Christianity, from the 5th century on, brought not only a script, but literary models which would in due course be transposed into Irish. It also involved a gradual shift from oral to written (Nagy, 1988). The argument for such influences rests on the introduction of regular rhymes and the quatrain form (see the Latin poems in Carney, 1985) whereas pre-Latin Irish poetry (and legal texts) made much stronger use of alliteration and rhythmic patterning (*roscada*). Whatever the degree of influence, even early Irish poetry sometimes shows an extraordinary degree of stylistic sophistication. Yeats' injunction to Irish poets to 'learn your trade' was certainly foreshadowed by these early practitioners, and there must have been systematic study of Irish grammar alongside that of Latin. Almost all the poetry in the period is syllabic (with unusually short lines of 7, 5, or 3 syllables) allied to complex patterns of rhyme or assonance. There may be links between the end of one stanza and the first line of the next (*aicill*) not to mention internal threads or echoes running across stanzas. (*Aicille* may be derived from the old Irish *aicillne*, meaning vassal-service, implying that the second rhyme was in service to the first!). The final line may return to the first, creating a form of closure (*dúnad*). Little wonder that the early scholars were fascinated by the sheer craft of what they were discovering, leading them sometimes to focus on form rather than content.

After this initial great burgeoning of work, research into early Irish poetry became less concerned with editing and translating *de novo*, and more with textual and contextual, especially historical, analysis. Although some important books of translations, noted below, appeared as the 20th century progressed, the emphasis in the long-running journals and scholarly literature was more on the interpretation of the material that had been unearthed. However, the main thrust has until recently been linguistic or historical rather than literary; a matter for criticism in Declan Kiberd's 'Foreword' to Ó Cathasaigh (2014). There is now a very large academic literature in the field which is constantly being added to and refined through continual challenge and re-interpretation. It is unlikely, though not impossible, that any new, original material will now be discovered.

So what of the content? It will have become clear from this collection, small as it is, that early Irish poetry varied a great deal, ranging from heroic, pagan or pagan-inspired narratives or panegyrics, through Christian homilies, prayers or reflections, to poems about the natural world (we should be cautious about calling them 'nature poems') which sometimes have a social subtext. There are some love poems, though not many, some of which were probably written by women. There are satirical poems, often the obverse of the panegyric. There is also a large category of poems of place – *dind/dinnseanchas* –

which celebrate a particular piece of topography and the people and stories associated with it.

Despite this great variety, several more general features of early Irish verse can be noted. First, as might be expected, it is largely a societal poetry, dealing with the common themes and shared ideas which were important to that society and helped bind it together: founding myths, history, genealogy, topography, key events, heroes and their stories. There are some more personal poems, some of which can seem remarkably accessible to us today, but they are very much in the minority, a point rather obscured by the fact that they tend to be the ones most often translated.

Secondly, and following on from this, it is often a poetry of naming, of people and places. The first is common enough in 'heroic' poetry in any culture, but the second is distinctive and manifests the particular Irish attachment to topography and locality. Another distinctive feature is the use of interjections or asides, or to give them their technical name, chevilles: 'I am telling you the truth'; 'Would I lie to you?' 'This is no trivial thing to say'; and so on. Any poet will understand the occasional need to complete a line somehow, and these chevilles were thus convenient, but they also make a direct link between poet and audience; one can almost see the meaningful look.

Perhaps the most important characteristic is also the one which makes this poetry doubly difficult to translate: its economy, and with that a kind of disciplined grace. Some of the poems here are miracles of compression, and early Irish writers seem to have taken to heart the notion that less is more. This compression should be understood in the context of a more general point, which is that early Irish poetry has no real epics: the long narratives or rather meandering stories, such as the best known old Irish text of *The Tain*, referred to later, are written mainly in prose, with periodic poetic effusions at charged moments. It is also worth pointing out that early Irish literature contains no drama.

Finally, it is important to note a methodological problem (see in particular Nos 4, 7, 28, 42, 63, 79,). Some longer texts consist of a combination of prose and verse ('prosimetric') in which cases it seems right to give due weight to each (see Mac Cana, 1997 and Note 42). But in other cases there exist short prose introductions or preambles to poems which may even occur in separate manuscripts. We sometimes do not know why or when these were written. While they may explain the context of a poem, it is also possible that they give it a particular spin which may or may not have been the intention of the poet. We need therefore to treat them with caution, even if not quite the hostility of O'Faoláin who regarded them as '...a scholastic trick, an effort, here, to swallow back the individual lyrists into the ossified traditions of the schools.' (1938: 146).

To return to the nativist/non-nativist issue: how one reads this poetry has, in the end, to be left up to the reader. Carney (1955) was not arguing simply that native Irish literature was influenced by Europe, but that it was part of a general, trans-actional European culture, with influences going both ways: for example, he has chapters on Irish elements in Tristan and Beowulf. His main concern is with narratives and indeed he only comments on one poem translated here (No 39) as part of a chapter on *Suibne Gelt* (Sweeney the Mad). There is a great variety of work contained in this book and I have sometimes ordered the poems to bring this out. Some poems lie quietly on the page, others cry out to be voiced. Some belong clearly within a Christian literary tradition while others evoke, sometimes nostalgically, a pagan ethos, even if they were penned by monks. I find others again difficult to place within either a nativist or European paradigm, representing a unique symbiosis.

SOURCES

I have drawn on two general sources in making this collection. The first is the van Hamel *Early Irish Poetry 600-1200* website which currently lists and gives references to close on 500 poems. I have also referred to various materials collected and edited as part of the University College Cork CELT project and a smaller project at the National University of Ireland in Dublin. None of these sites is exhaustive, and some of the poems included here have been found elsewhere. Muireann Ní Bhrolcháin's *An Introduction to Early Irish Literature* (2009) gives a good overview of the period, in particular the various literary cycles, with a final chapter on poets and poetry, but we still surprisingly lack a comprehensive book on early Irish poetry.

As regards specific sources, I have used mainly the originals collected in Ernst Windisch's and Whitley Stokes' *Irische Texte mit Wörterbuch* (referred to below as IT); Whitley Stokes' and John Strachan's *Thesaurus Paleohibernicus*, Vol. 2 (referred to as TP); Kuno Meyer's *Four Old-Irish Songs of Summer and Winter* (KM) and *Bruchstücke der älteren Lyrik Irlands* (BL); Gerard Murphy's *Early Irish Lyrics* (EIL), James Carney's *Medieval Irish Lyrics and the Irish Bardic Poet* (MIL) and David Greene and Frank O'Connor's *A Golden Treasury of Irish Poetry AD600-1200*. Most of the older sources are now available online (see in particular the website archive.org). As regards the language, my main resources have been the grammars of Thurneysen (1975, first published 1946) and Stifter (2006). I have made extensive use of the on-line version of the Royal Irish Academy's *Dictionary of the Irish Language* (www.dil.ie) and referred occasionally to Dinneen's dictionary to check modern meanings (Dinneen, 1965). Almost all the poems here have been translated before, some several times, and I have looked at these versions. In particular I have consulted Kuno Meyer's *Ancient Irish Poetry*; Robin Flower's *The Irish Tradition*; Greene and O'Connor (see above); Frank O'Connor's *Kings Lords and Commons*; Kenneth Jackson's *A Celtic Miscellany*; *The Faber Book of Irish Verse* (ed. John Montague); and Myles Dillon's *Early Irish Literature*. I have cross-checked some poems with those in the *Field Day Anthology of Irish Writing* (Deane, 1991; Bourke, 2005). The most recent general anthology (*The Penguin Book of Irish Poetry*, edited by Patrick Crotty, 2012) has a substantial selection of early Irish poetry, although just 28 of the 80 I have translated coincide, and 31 in Maurice Riordan's anthology *The Finest Music*, published in 2014. For readings of the originals of Nos. 11, 32 and 72 go to the ASNC Spoken Word website.

Translation implies a contract between translator and reader that there is some justifiable relationship between the original and what is being offered. I have tried therefore to spell out my approach in some detail below. Some readers will approve of it, others will likely disapprove. Either way they may want to know what a literal prose translation or paraphrase would look like, in which case they should turn to Gerard Murphy's *Early Irish Lyrics* (1956) which in my view still provides the most consistently faithful English renditions of the originals, and which include about a quarter of the 80 poems in this book, thus offering a substantial basis for comparison. (I have divided one poem into two: Nos. 41/42.)

Approaches to translation range from attempts to reproduce the first language in the second, to attempts to find equivalences or parallels between them. One problem with trying to reproduce the Irish in English has already been mentioned: whereas Irish (almost always) has a VSO (verb-subject-object) word order, English has SVO. Secondly, as Stifter (2006: 16) points out there are 50% more phonemes in old Irish than in modern English (66 as against 44) despite a smaller alphabet. Thirdly, there is a long-established distinction in linguistics between analytic and synthetic languages. This was originally formulated by Schlegel and later refined by Sapir and others (Sapir, E. (1921) *Language: an Introduction to the Study of Speech*. New York: Harcourt, Brace and Co.). It is a complex distinction because as Greene (1973) has pointed out not only may languages contain aspects of both but they may also change over time. But to summarise, in analytic languages words tend to have one invariant form, and meaning is built up by creating strings of them, making word order very important. In synthetic languages, words can take multiple forms, and meaning is constructed by declining, conjugating, inflecting or otherwise modifying them. At the extreme, a single word in a synthetic language could correspond to a whole sentence in an analytic one, although in practice the distinction is better seen as a spectrum.

Modern English is relatively analytic. True, we can add 's' to make a plural noun, or 'ing' to make a participle. But on the whole, we have to add more words – articles, pronouns, prepositions, compound verbs – to build up meanings. Old Irish, by contrast, is relatively synthetic. Words may change not only at the beginning (affixes) and end (suffixes) but in the middle, so that what is expressed in several words in English may be covered by a single word in Irish. For example verbs conjugate (as in Latin) and the genitive case is typically formed by inserting an 'i' in the noun. This makes the language relatively compressed and economical, with the result that translating it into English often involves using more words and thus longer lines, although the key measure in poetry is syllables rather than words.

Translating Irish verse into English verse brings added problems. There exist clear and useful literal translations or paraphrases of many of these originals. There is however a sense that something is lost in these. The issue can be seen more clearly by turning it round. If I was given a piece of foreign prose to translate, and did so into verse, people would likely think I was mad. What is added, or in reverse, taken away? I have drawn a distinction elsewhere between what poems say and what they do (Squires, 2010: 38-46). The latter comprises what we refer to broadly as 'form': the complex of line, metre, alliteration, rhyme and assonance that poetry involves.

Since form is a key and sometimes contentious issue, it may be useful to step back a moment and ask the functional question: what is form for? There are perhaps three main answers. First, form has a mnemonic function in that features such as alliteration, rhythm and rhyme make a poem easier to remember, something that was especially important in a culture with limited written resources. Secondly, form provides the psychic satisfactions of pattern and closure that, for example, Gestalt psychology explores. Thirdly, form can reinforce meaning. The iambics of 'the curfew tolls the knell of parting day' fit the sense like a glove, accentuating the important words and gliding over the lesser ones.

These three functions also help us to understand the difference between regular and free verse. Regular verse involves all three, although sometimes the demands of the first and second can constrain or distort the third. Free verse, by contrast, rests entirely on the third: what the verse does must stem directly from what it says. This requirement means that, as Eliot noted, it is not 'free' at all; as the famous opening lines of *The Waste Land* demonstrate, it must embody or enact the sense precisely. It is not easier to compose, simply difficult in a different way.

None of these functions is an absolute: each can be performed in various ways and to varying degrees. Form is sometimes seen as a criterion or end in itself, becoming a kind of poetic fetish (something that arguably contributed to the eventual decline of Irish bardic poetry). It is not: what matters is that the poem satisfies us in terms of recall, pattern and the fit of sound and sense. It seems reasonable thus to expect poetry to be translated into poetry, like into like. However, the competing and sometimes conflicting demands of the forms in the two languages place additional demands on the translator. Trying to reproduce the original rhyme scheme in a second language can lead to forced rhymes or contorted syntax which then defeat the underlying aim of creating something like poetry. Poetic forms belong to their own language and when we translate we thus have to find an equivalent in the second language. Attempts to mimic Irish forms in English can lead to a kind of faux-Celt prosody which is neither one thing nor the other. See also David Ferry's approach to translating Virgil's *Georgics*, New York: FSG, 2005, pp. xix-xx.

There are two specific issues with the translations here. First, as just noted, my English translations tend to come out a bit longer than the originals in terms of the number of syllables (as do routinely the English versions of the translation exercises in Stifter, 2006). Irish grammar is extremely complex, so it is difficult to generalise, but one can suggest some possible reasons for this. There is no indefinite article in Irish and the definite article occurs less frequently in the poetry than in English. There are no relative pronouns (that, which, who, etc.) in Irish. Whereas tenses in Irish are generally created through verbal inflections, in English they usually involve an additional word (have, will, should, etc.). Old Irish makes great use of 'preverbs' (preposition-like words which precede the verb, cf 'outdo', 'overhear') but some of these elide syllables in the verbal stem, although some tenses have 'augmented' stems. Infixed pronouns in Irish often simply add a letter, not a syllable. The one-syllable Irish *dúib* requires 'for you' in English, and the same is true of other conjugated prepositions (Stifter, 2006: 89-90). The common –ly English adverb adds a syllable and the –able/-ible adjective adds two. Latinate words in English are often polysyllabic. As the original and translation of No 22 show, the three-syllable line of the Irish usually comes out as four or five in English. And the classic seven-syllable line may come out as nine or ten. This relates to the second problem.

Although the earliest poems are accentual, most of the originals here are written in syllabic rather than metrical verse: one simply counts out the syllables to measure the line. However, syllabic verse is rare in English and has no historical roots. Not only that, even where it exists, it may be read accentually. Robin Flower's translation of Pangur Ban reproduces the seven-syllable lines of the original:

> *I and Pangur Bán my cat   'tis a like task we are at*

However, the English reader is likely to hear these as tetrameters, so ingrained is accent in English. There are about 60 basic, monosyllabic, unaccented articles, pronouns, prepositions, conjunctions and tenses in English which alone would make it accentual. This is not to rule out the potential value of syllabic verse as counter-intuitive, surprising and arresting. But the longer the line, I would suggest, the more difficult it is to keep it syllabic and prevent it falling aurally into the inherited accentual patterns of English poetry.

Rhyme is, on the face of it, less of a problem. The two most common Irish rhyme schemes are *rannaigecht*, rhyming b/d, and *deibide*, rhyming a/b and c/d. There are variants of each of these, but they correspond broadly to similar rhyme schemes in English. However, two points should be made. First, what counts as rhyme in Irish is not always what our modern Anglophone ears would register as such; the rules were simply different, and depend partly on stress. Secondly, there is the issue of how rhyme is perceived. In times when it was the norm in poetry, it was perhaps less striking than it is now, when it exists against a background of widespread free verse. Rightly or wrongly, I sometimes find it too obvious, too clinching, and have gone for half-rhyme or assonance instead.

My approach has varied from poem to poem. In a few cases, I think I have come close to reproducing the form of the Irish. However, in the majority, I have gone for something equivalent, typically employing short lines, some alliteration, occasional rhyme and a good deal of assonance. As can be seen from the originals at the end, this is not usually quite the same as the Irish, but to me the demands of poetry outweigh those of similitude. (For an attempt directly to reproduce the Irish, see Ruth Lehmann's *Early Irish Verse*, University of Texas, 1982; an attempt which Alan Harrison in *Irish University Review* (Spring 1983) regards as misconceived; and I have to agree). Translation is not a purely linguistic enterprise; it is cultural also, in that both texts are embedded in their contexts, and I have tried to respect both. This also helps to explain why translations often date; they are inevitably to some degree products of their own time and place.

Another aspect of the poems concerns the relative emphasis on the oral and the written. Some of them seem to me private jottings, while others cry out to be spoken aloud and probably were. The poetry of the period ranges from glosses and marginalia on the one hand to panegyric bardic verse on the other. I hope I have not over-voiced some of them, but I think scholars sometimes perceive such work as purely written, in the form in which it has come down to us, and miss the element of voicing. This can lead to an over-emphasis on some aspects of prosody rather than others.

As I worked on these poems I realised that some belonged to the pagan, heroic or mythical tradition and others to the world of Irish Christianity. I thought about arranging the poems in two chronological groups to reflect this, but in the end decided against it because at the time the two were intermingled. Initially the Irish church, like all new religions tend to, built on, assimilated and adapted much that was there already.

The hagiography of its saints represents a curious mixture of Christian and pagan elements. But even by the end of the period in question, when Christianity had become firmly established, there were still poets and no doubt others who harked back to the misty, mythical times. Irish saints too were putatively involved in the oral, pagan traditions. One text, the *Acallamh na Senórach*, has St. Patrick engaging in an extended dialogue with long-dead heroes. St. Columba was said to have saved the (as ever) troublesome poets from wholesale exile (see Nagy, 1997). So it was in many ways a symbiotic culture, in which the two strands had become subtly intertwined and I therefore decided to reflect this in the mix and sequence of the poems. They are not in chronological order, even if I knew what the chronology was.

Another issue which faces every translator is the relationship between denotative and connotative meanings: the dictionary definition and the wider associations that a word may have. Poetry, I would suggest, depends heavily on the latter, which gives it much of its richness, and I have therefore erred on the side of inclusion in translating the meanings of some words, on the grounds that the listeners at the time would have 'heard' their full resonance. Even in some of the 'nature' poems one sometimes picks up a social subtext, and in some of the overtly pious ones, there is an element of wit and play. Perhaps for these reasons, the gap of time and place that exists between our world and theirs seems somehow less than one might expect it to be.

That said, we need to be cautious in our assumptions that what the writers meant is what we understand. Translations have a habit of dating quickly, so that each age has to redo the job. This is surely because translators unconsciously and inevitably bring something of their own culture to the task. The trap is most dangerous when we are using ideas which seem familiar or unproblematic: notions such as 'nature', 'community' or 'country'. Conversely, concepts such as 'nobility', 'obedience' or 'triumph' pose an obvious challenge. The only general point I would make is that it is best to try to let the poems speak for themselves rather than imposing preconceptions or stereotypes to do with 'the Celtic world' on them, notions which may say as much about us as it. Even in this short selection, the poems exhibit a considerable variety of content and tone. Some of them are surprisingly fresh and accessible, others definitely alien, very much of their own time. The mix of poems in itself poses challenges. Although the earliest poems are different in terms of prosody, relying more on repetition and alliteration than syllabics and rhyme, the problem is not primarily a chronological one. Rather, it reflects the different nature and content of the verse. The heroic, warrior poems are very different from the reflective, spiritual ones or the gentler 'nature' poems. Some poems are repetitive or formulaic, something that can seem strange to the modern reader. The 7/5/7/5 stanza form gives some of them special pace and momentum. The short satirical poems have to be sharp. Quatrains pose their own, compact, challenge. Rather than trying to establish or find a common 'voice' or style, I have endeavoured to bring out the contrasting strengths of the different genres, to display the extraordinary range of the writing.

One question which must be left hanging here is the influence of this verse on subsequent Irish poetry, whether the *Dánta Grádha* (love poems) of the 14th to 17th centuries (see Ó Rathile, 1926; Young, 1975) the great Munster laments of the 17th and 18th (see Corkery, 1924; Ó Tuama and Kinsella, 1981), the 19th and 20th century 'Celtic Revival' or indeed contemporary writing. Some anthologies (e.g. Deane, 1991; Bourke, 2005; Crotty, 2012) see a unity or continuity of tradition; I am not so sure. One problem is that much of the early work translated here was simply not available to later writers until the great project of recovering it began towards the end of the 19th century. Another is the major political and social changes that happened in the centuries after 1200, most of which imply discontinuity rather than continuity. And while the nativist/ non-nativist debate is a live one in relation to medieval poetry in terms of the impact of Latin, it is also a subsequent issue in terms of the influence of foreign models, whether European court poetry, romanticism or the various literary movements of the modern age.

However, as noted in the Preface, I do think this work can still speak to us. Whether it does is another matter: I recently remarked to an Irish colleague that even well-read Irish people probably don't know more than a dozen of these poems, and he replied: if that. And this work will I think be 'news' to most other people in the English-speaking world.

The historical and linguistic emphasis of much Celtic scholarship in the past has perhaps unintentionally margin-alised a literary perspective, which focuses more on the content and significance of these poems, both in their own time and for us now. Such a perspective has however to negotiate a complex and subtle interplay of relationship and difference, identification and otherness. We cannot simply 'assimilate' this work to our own perspectives and values: that would be too easy. But neither should we consign it wholly and safely to the past, as if it meant nothing to people now. I hope that this book will, along with others, help us to engage with early Irish poetry as literature, indeed what Goethe called *Weltliteratur*, belonging not just to Ireland but to the world.

IV. Textual Notes

There are two main problems in annotating these poems. The first is that, as already pointed out, we still lack, even after 130 years of scholarship, a comprehensive book on early Irish poetry that would allow us to locate and relate these texts. The second is that existing general histories of early Irish literature tend to be organised around the four main cycles – Mythological, Heroic, Fenian and Kings (see for example Ní Bhrolcháin, 2009; Ó Cathasaigh, 2014, chapter 1). These are actually of limited use in understanding the range of poems presented here which would require some different form of classification, yet to be devised. Many of these poems deserve a monograph to themselves, and a few have one. The references cited here therefore constitute only a small proportion of those that exist and an even smaller one of what would ideally be available.

For the sake of brevity, I refer to stanzas as S1, 2 etc and lines as a, b, c, d. I have given the beginning of the first line in Irish in each case, and two (simplified) points about reading these can be made. First, an acute accent (*fada*) lengthens the vowel. Secondly the presence of an *h* typically softens or even elides the immediately preceding consonant. However, it should be noted that Old Irish spelling was quite variable, as was the use of accents. For example the orthography of the first line of No 2 differs in each of the five sources.

The sources listed here usually begin with the earliest printed ones which I have consulted, which in turn refer back to the manuscripts. Where relevant, I have used the abbreviated forms of references given in the Sources and tried to keep the process as concise as possible.

1. *Ticfa táilcenn...* (Whitley Stokes (1887) *The Tripartite Life of Patrick*, London, HMSO, p. 1 (i.e. 50); MIL, p. 2; Nagy, 1997, p. 46). Carney believes this very early poem to be probably 6th c. The adze was a curved cutting instrument, here referring rudely to the distinctive tonsure of the Irish monks. I have come across the epithet in several other poems, suggesting it was quite common; see McCarthy (2003). The poem is assumed to be about the coming of the 5th century St. Patrick, written after the event in the form of a prophecy before it, possibly by a hostile druid. The stick is a bishop's crozier, and the scene is that of a Mass. Interestingly, a Latin translation of the poem was made in the seventh century, which incidentally helped Carney (1985: 97) to reconstruct tentatively a line missing from the Irish text (5th line, my 6th). The poem is also quoted in Ó Cróinín (1995: 32). When I read this poem at a festival someone commented afterwards that it felt like a curse, and I think the old pagan formula of repetition (here of *ceann*, head) has a strange and disturbing effect. One of the problems in translating the poem is that all our vocabulary for blasphemy or impiety is from the Christian angle, whereas here it is Christianity that is alien and impious. It is difficult to get one's head round that, but this was the reality in pagan Ireland: Patrick and his like were seen as interlopers, a threat to the well-established spiritual and social order which had perhaps been in place already for as long as 500 years. On the relationship between the old and new religions see chapter 3 in Bhreathnach (2014).

2. *Cá lín trícha a n-Éirinn áin...* (Eugene O'Curry (1855) *Cath Mhuighe Léana/The Battle of Magh Leana*, Celtic Society, Dublin.) Stanzas 1-11. The poem is discussed in Hogan (1928/9). For a description and diagram of territorial units see MacCotter (2008) who explains (p. 49ff) that the *tricha cét* had four functions: (1) a unit of royal tenure, (2) a unit of local government and law enforcement, (3) a unit for tax collection and (4) a unit of military levy. He also makes the important point that measurements were based on arable land not all land, so that the size of units varied considerably, being much larger in the less fertile west than the lusher parts of Leinster. The origins of this poem are obscure. The earliest manuscript is in the *Book of Ui Maine* which was compiled in the 1390s.

However, that contains some older material, and the *nd* spelling of *Eirind* in the poem there points to something a good deal earlier. The fact that Charles-Edwards (2000) does not mention the *baile* at all in his detailed account of communal structures around 700AD suggests that they belonged to an earlier, if here imagined, age. (Thurneysen (1975: 245) notes the habit of expressing large numbers in smaller combinations.) Here, the *tricha cét* (thirty hundreds) was originally a military phrase referring to the number of men that could be raised by a territory; for example, in the *Táin* (see No 4) the renegade Ulsterman Fergus has a troop of three thousand. However over time it came to refer merely to the geographical area. Although it is not quite the same as the old territorial unit, I have translated *baile* as 'townland' (in modern Irish, *baile tír*) which is still a unit in the Irish countryside; they vary in size but the one I grew up in was probably about three square miles. One writer (Toner) has suggested that 'settlement' would be a better term, but its use here seems more demarcated than that; a *baile biataig* was a collection of farmers and specifically those who could produce food sufficient to provide for travelling kings or officials. Toner (2004) also states that the earliest uses of *baile* are in the 11th or early 12th century, which would support the view that this is a Middle Irish poem. In early Ireland, Meath was sometimes seen as a distinct entity, being the locus of the capital at Tara, and Munster was divided into two provinces. The provinces of Ireland were commonly described as 'fifths'. Early Irish poetry was much concerned with topography and geography; for example there is a poem in the *Liber Hymnorum* listing the five parts of Munster. In the first line here *Éirinn áin* was a stock phrase rather like *la belle France*; I have used 'island' to avoid repeating 'Ireland' in the second stanza. Richter (2005: 9) notes that even in early times the country was perceived emotionally as a whole, something evident in this poem. In S1b *go m-baidh* is unclear but the DIL *báid* (b) gives the meaning of pact or alliance. In S1c it is possible that *comall n-glé* is simply a cheville, with *glé* providing a useful final monosyllable. Confusingly *cumall* means the value of three milch cows. However the DIL gives 'fair assembly' for the phrase and I think the meaning here is of a clear array. I have thus paraphrased it as 'side by side' which also carries the positive tone of the poem with its evocation of a harmonious whole. In S1d I take *coingebus* to be a compound of *cuinge,* meaning yoke or frame, and the word for cattle (medieval Irish cattle went *bú* not moo!). It probably refers to a *cuinge sesrige,* the common ploughing team of six. I initially translated S2b *go n'ilar séd* as 'teeming with deer' which with the previous reference to cattle seemed plausible. However, on reflection I suspect that *séd* here is a variant of *sét*, a word which occurs in the 8th century legal tract *Críth Gablach* and which can be translated as 'chattels' (MacNeill, 1923: 284). The *sét* had a specified value (equivalent to a heifer or half a milch cow) which was used not only to estimate wealth but also as a measure of compensation for victims of wrong-doing. *Inver Dublin* was the old name for the town at the mouth of the River Liffey. In the following line, *bóroimhe* is a compound of the word for cow and the verb to count (*airem*). It refers to the practice of kings of taking droves of cattle as tribute from their underlings and a pass (*bealach*) probably in the west of Leinster where this happened. King Brian Boru may have earned this epithet because of his penchant for doing this. I have taken the various chevilles to refer to accuracy/error rather than lies/falsehood. The picture presented here is of an island at peace with itself, in contrast to the battles (probably often skirmishes) recounted in the various historical cycles. Fintan was a mythical Irish poet who figures in the *Lebor Gabála Érenn*, the 11th century account of the history of Ireland from the Flood until historical times, and preserved in the Book of Leinster among other places (see the edition and translation with that title by R. A. Stewart Macalister, published by the Irish Texts Society, Dublin, 1937-42.) Although parts of the LGE may echo actual events, it is largely mythological, as is Fintan who after accompanying Noah's grand-daughter to Ireland, lived on for several thousand years through the various invasions or migrations; he makes several appearances in the literature: see Nagy, 1997: 4-7. The style of this poem is indeed similar to many in the LGE, with their emphasis on names, lists and enumeration. This raises the possibility that it is a stray from the LGE (and the *Book of Ui Maine* does contain some LGE texts) but since the latter was widely-known in its day, it is equally possible that the style was simply copied. In S3b, O'Curry translates *an fer go céill* as 'the man of sense'. However, in legend, Fintan is always described as 'the wise' and I have used that.

3. *Fritha gach da chosmuilius...* (Meyer, K. (1897) *Zeitschrift für celtische Philologie (ZCP)*, 1, 112). Meyer classifies this poem as Middle Irish and gives the manuscript reference as Eg. 1782, fo. 56a, 2. However it is difficult to date. The Latin loanword *saxain* initially meant Saxon and then later more broadly English, and is the root of the modern Irish *Sasana* (and Scottish *Sassanach*). It occurs in the 12th century *Book of the Dun Cow*, but possibly earlier also. *Francta,* another Latin loanword, originally meant north German tribes but probably refers more generally here to mainland Europe and modern France. The range of foreign references in the poem suggests something quite late, but the provincial stereotypes go back a long way (the reference to the O'Neills, who dominated western Ulster, is of little help in dating since they were the most long-lasting of all Irish dynastic families, supposedly originating in the 5th century and still important in Elizabethan times). This and the previous poem exemplify the early Irish emphasis on place and locality, something which is true even in today's much more urbanised country: people sometimes still refer to the *seanfhóide* (the 'oul sod'). In the past, this attachment and identity would have been reinforced by localised conflicts between largely autonomous peoples (*túatha*) or fiefdoms: Irish kings (*rí* or *ruarí*) could be local, regional or national and the term is relative. Many of the poems listed on the van Hamel site are *dinnseanchas* (*dind/dinn* means 'notable place' and *seanchas* 'old stories/tales/lore/traditions') and the CELT website has the entire collection of metrical dinnseanchas assembled and translated by E.W. Gwynn at the beginning of the 20th century; see also the main van Hamel list. I find most of them of little poetic merit, but readers can judge for themselves. This poem is however an interesting example of contemporary stereotyping. Stereotypes are a wider issue in the Celtic field. People at the time did not use the word 'celt' and it was not until the 17th/18th centuries that the links between the various Celtic languages were recognised. From there, the idea of a distinct Celtic culture gradually developed in the 19th and 20th centuries, characterised by certain stereo-

types, some positive (imaginative, spiritual, close to nature) some negative (irrational, primitive, marginal). The subject is discussed in Terence Brown's *Celticism* (1996) which brings together a collection of essays on archaeology, history and literature. The book was apparently inspired by a (rather uncritical) reading of Edward Said's *Orientalism* and the general message, as with Said, is that such stereotypes were ultimately disabling, and helped to legitimate colonialism. However the term 'celtic' is widely used in academic circles: there is an International Congress of Celtic Studies (ICCS) and a Celtic Studies Association of North America (CSANA) under whose auspices rigorous research and scholarship are carried out. The relevant question here is perhaps a reflexive one: what associations or expectations, if any, does the word have for the reader, and how do these stand up to the encounter with the texts?

4. *Atchiu fer find firfes chless...* (Dunn, J. (1914) *The Ancient Irish Epic Tale Táin Bó Cúalnge*, London, David Nutt: 17-18; Cecile O'Rahilly (1967) *Táin Bó Cúailnge* (the Cattle Raid of Cooley) from the *Book of Leinster*, Dublin: Dublin Institute for Advanced Studies; also CELT edition of the latter). There are two recensions and numerous editions and translations: see the van Hamel site. This is the nearest early Irish has to an epic, recounted in a mixture of prose and poetry, and which has generated a substantial literature on its own. It been translated by various people including the poets Thomas Kinsella and Ciaran Carson. This poem occurs near the beginning of the tale. Medb (Maeve) queen of Connaught, who comes across as a jealous and impulsive woman, cannot bear the fact that she and her husband Ailill are equal in wealth except that he possesses a famous white bull. Medb has people scour the country to find a comparable animal and eventually one is located in Cooley (Co. Louth). She decides to have it, by negotiation or by force if necessary, and raises an army. Here the prophetess Feidelm is warning her not to attack the Ulstermen led by their hero Cú Chulainn who appears to her in this vision; Medb goes ahead despite the dire predictions. Ulster here refers to the south-eastern part of the modern province, centred on Armagh. The driving regularity of the original, reinforced by some repetition (*fail... fail...*)

gives it much of its power; by contrast, I have used varying line lengths to try to capture some of this. I have doubled up on the meanings of *finn* in the first line. In 1b, one version has *chret* (body) rather than *créchta* (wounds) and it is surprising that wounds spoil the otherwise perfect picture; on the other hand, they accentuate Cú Chulainn's bravery. The reference to appearing in another form may refer to part of the tale where he is temporarily transformed into a warlike monster; in his translation of *The Tain* Kinsella (1969) dramatises this in the poem: 'the Warped Man deals death/that fair form I first beheld/melted to a mis-shape'. Cú Chulainn became known as the hound (*cú*) because as a boy he killed a fierce guard hound which was about to attack him; he promised to act thereafter as guardian of the province. The various stories about Cú Chulainn are told in the Ulster cycle (see Ní Bhrolcháin 2009: 41-55). As Ó Cróinín (1995: 59ff) notes, there is much less material about Connaught than the other provinces, and no distinct literary cycle. History being written by the victors, one wonders if that has affected our view of Medb and the Connaught cause. It is important to distinguish between warriors such as Cú Chulainn who represented a people (here of Ulster) and those such as Finn and the *fiana* who fought mainly on their own account and were really marauding bands of outlaws despite their modern adoption as national, emblematic heroes (see Nos 14, 44, 45). Ó Murchadha (2009: xxi) notes that the word *fiana* may derive from the Latin word for hunting, *venatio*. In Modern Irish it is spelled with two 'n's.

5. *Admuiniur secht n-ingena trethan...* (Meyer, K. (1914) 'An old Irish prayer for long life' in Elton, O. (ed.) *A Miscellany presented to John Macdonald Mackay*. Liverpool University Press/London: Constable). See also the editions/translations by Greene and O'Connor (1990) and Carey (2000). The poem is attributed to the abbot of Comraire in Meath, Fer Fio, who died in 762. The overtly Christian conclusion in Latin comes oddly after what seems like a mainly pagan incantation, including a number of now incomprehensible references, and the poem suggests a gradual blending of the two cultures. The mention of 'rounds' (my 'travels') is perhaps consistent with an abbot's pastoral responsibilities. I have translated *laisrén* as flashing but as noted by Carey it might refer to an earlier saint of that

name. *Ní nascar mo chlú ar chel*: I am unsure whether this is a statement or a wish, but given the surrounding *ní* forms have opted for the latter. I think *chlú* refers to the speaker's concern for his reputation as a holy man and that he should not lose this (*chel* means to become extinct, or die) hence 'endure'. The DIL suggests that *findruine* might mean electrum, a by-product of the smelting of gold and silver, but also cites 'white bronze'. The latter is not actually bronze but an attractive alloy of copper, tin and zinc and although I am not sure that the last would have been available I have decided to go with that translation. To me, the general evocation of metals in this passage has a quasi-magical ring. *Ro sóerthar mo recht* has been translated in various ways, but I think refers to rights or status. *Ním-ragba nathir díchuinn/ná doirb dúrglas/ná doel díchuinn*: the various translations and even transcriptions of these lines (Thurneysen in Stokes and Windisch, 1891; Meyer, 1914; Greene and O'Connor, 1990; Carey, 2000) all differ. I take the *ui* of *díchuinn* to be the genitive of the 'o' in *conn*; *cenn* in the genitive or dative becomes *ciunn* (Thurneysen, 1975: 47). Thus I have rejected the translations of headless or two-headed in favour of one which focuses on God-given human sense or reason (*conn*) in contrast to the natural world. However, it is possible that this was originally a pagan text which became Christianised, and that the original reference was to *cenn*; and one can see how *iu* might easily be mistranscribed as *ui*. (However, an evil hag visiting the legendary King Conaire Mór included *díchuinne* among her long string of names: see Bitel, 1996: 210). The poem is irregular, but makes considerable use of rhyme and of course repetition. Rhythmically alliterative speech was called *roscada* (see also No. 9).

6. *Deargrúathar cloinne Morna...* (Murphy, G. (1933) *Duanaire Finn*, Irish Texts Society, London, Vol II.) I have translated the first 10 stanzas of the 39 in poem XLVIII in the sequence. *ca.* 1400? See also Ó Murchadha (2009) *Lige Guill: the grave of Goll*, London: Irish Texts Society, esp. pp. 88-91. The latter poem occurs in the *Book of Leinster*, but because it did not form part of the diplomatic edition nor of Gwynn's collected *dinnseanchas* was not edited or easily available until this recent study which prints and edits both *Lige Guill* and *Deargrúathar cloinne Morna*, making it easy to compare them.

LG probably originated in the 11th century, perhaps after the bitter provincial wars that followed the death of Brian Boru. It is of course set in mythical times and based on the enmity between Goll of Morna and Finn of the Baíscne, but it may also reflect the contemporary tensions between Connaught and Leinster. Of the ten DCM stanzas (out of 39) translated here, seven correspond substantially with LG which has 86 stanzas in all: 1:48; 2:49; 3:50; 4:12; 8:51; 9:62; 10:56/57. Stanzas 5-7 do not correspond although some names are the same. The later author has deliberately used some archaic forms, presumably to give an impression of antiquity. Ó Murchadha (p. 77) describes DCM as 'a version of, or at least a poem deeply indebted to, *Lige Guill*'. He has little to say about the literary nature of LG, beyond calling it 'bloodthirsty', but provides a detailed analysis of the similarities and differences between the two versions, noting that the later one is much less accomplished technically. I had in fact already translated DCM before getting hold of LG and although I tried to translate the roughly corresponding stanzas 48-57 of LG, they do not work as well. I have therefore decided to stay with DCM. This is unsatisfactory in that it goes beyond my chosen period and as a matter of principle I prefer to use the oldest versions. The problem is that DCM makes for the better translation: it begins in a striking way, uses repetition effectively, builds the momentum steadily, culminating in the three Aodh's, and comes to rest (literally) with Caoinche. I have however corrected four misreadings (according to Ó Murchadha) in S1c, d; S4b; S9a; and S10d, bringing it somewhat closer to LG. In S1f, Cliodna may refer to Glandore in Co. Cork, whose waves (*tonn*) were famous. (There is a clear progression from north to south in LG.) In S7d, Aillbhe is a name but might also have become a place-name, which would make the burning less shocking; however, S7 in LG refers to the slaying of Cuilenn and Ailbe and there are other references to people being incinerated. In all this is, to my mind, one of the most powerful war poems I know, made more so by the occasional personal references, which are stronger in DCM than LG. The very thing that makes this poem difficult to read in English – the roll-call of names – is what gives it its cumulative power. (See the Glossary for pronunciations.) These longer poems, including the next one, raise structural issues for the translator. It was clearly important at the time to enumerate and name people and places and to recount the details of battles, perhaps as a matter of record, perhaps out of respect for the warrior ethos: respect which could also extend sometimes to the enemy: LG begins by describing Goll as a 'kingly warrior' (*rígnía)* and says that his unattended grave should be given daily protection. (One might relate this to our 'conventions' of war.) However, in a modern poem such lists can seem repetitive and tedious. I want my translations to read naturally as poems in English, so I have excluded much of this detail; but I would exhort readers who want to get a true sense of the originals to absorb these notes and then turn to scholarly studies such as Ó Murchadha's. On the Fenian cycle generally see Arbuthnot and Parsons (2011).

7. *A ben náchamaicille...* (Meyer, K. (1910) *Fianaigecht: being a collection of hitherto inedited Irish poems and tales related to Finn and his Fiana,* Todd Lecture Series, Hodges Figgis, London; reprinted in his *Ancient Irish Poetry,* p. 9.) For the original see the CELT website. For another, verse translation see O'Faoláin (1938) and for a text and prose translation see Greene and O'Connor. I am also grateful to Kristen Mills for sight of an article exploring gender aspects of the text. 8th or 9th century. The poem is usually known as the *Reicne Fothaid Canainne* (see below). There are two prose introductions, one in old and one in middle Irish, telling how Fothad, a Connaught chieftain, rejected his own wife after falling in love with the more beautiful wife of a Munster chief. She was prepared to leave her husband but demanded a high price in gold, silver and bronze, which Fothad agreed to, promising half the rivets in his comrades' weapons; hence the perhaps bitter reference to 'spoils'. In the ensuing battle, Fothad is killed and the poem is (probably) spoken by his decapitated head. While both introductions refer to the woman carrying the head, in the poem it is simply lying on the ground. (As noted earlier, it is difficult to know how much weight to place on prose introductions generally, since they may give a particular spin to the interpretation.) My translation is of stanzas 1-10, omitting No 7 which suddenly and temporarily reverts to the third person voice of the introduction; then, following

Greene and O'Connor, stanza 23; and the final stanzas 40-49. The rest of the poem comprises a detailed description of the battle and then a list of Fothad's possessions, the 'spoils'. Such description and enumeration are typical of early Irish poetry and it is interesting to ask why. One reason perhaps is that poetry was one of the main forms of social memory, a way of recording events at a time when there were few others. The second is that these were ultimately praise poems. We do not know who wrote this poem, but it is likely to have been someone associated with the clan, at the time or later. The point of describing the feats of battle was to show how heroic the warriors were; the point of listing the spoils was to emphasise how affluent Fothaid and his family were. So these features were very much of their time, though they do not add much to the essential story; readers can turn to Meyer for the full text if they wish. There is also a mention of the dreaded goddess of battle, Morrígan, who often took the form of a woman or a crow, and about whom there is a substantial literature, plus a rather conventional Christian invocation at the end. On the various forms and manifestations of war goddesses see Carey (1983) and although his article does not specifically refer to this poem Egeler (2008) explores parallels between Irish battlefield demons and similar phenomena in other cultures. The poem is complex and there are various issues. The term *reicne* is sometimes translated as 'lament' but was actually a more general term for a poem; for a discussion of the genre of lament see Hollo (2005). In stanza 23, *úath* could be translated as 'horror' or 'terror'. The first implies the earthly horrors of the aftermath of the battle, the second the unearthly terror of the ghosts of the dead; on the latter see Borsje (2007). However, I have preferred O Faoláin's 'dread' as capturing also the sense of the unknown. (While all three nouns remain powerful, their adjectives have become weak.) The poem is interesting both in its evocation of the warrior ethos and relationships with women (e.g. the tension between 'fault' and 'cause'). In the original stanza 41 Meyer's text has *fodercc bol* which he translates as 'famous luck'. However, Greene and O'Connor translate their *forderg bal* as 'bloody appearance' and my 'bloodstained' follows that. There is also a supernatural element towards the end of the poem, and the reference in the original stanzas 41 and 42 to the Morrigan 'washing' entrails and spoils is problematic. Given the general context of the poem, I first translated this as ' many and dreadful the entrails/that the Morrigan bathes in blood' but I have found nothing in the text or elsewhere to support this, although washing in blood does have Satanic associations and blood and water are our two primary fluids. The reference is probably to the well-known legend of the 'washer at the ford' (Schoepperle, 1919, who cites part of the poem at the end; see also Carey, 2000). In this, some men come upon a woman washing blood-stained weapons and sometimes also gore at a ford and ask her whose they are. She replies 'yours' thus foretelling their deaths. Although both the story and the poem employ the same verb for washing (*nigim*) the reference in the poem is anomalous in that it is concurrent, not premonitory. (There is a mention of a raven picking at entrails in the *Fingal Ronáin*, No. 42). It is also a little odd that the reference to the Morrigan begins abruptly in mid-stanza. The poet may have conflated the two stories simply to add to the general horror, although the initial reference to the unwashed head confusingly refers to the ritual washing of the dead.

8. *Trí meic Ruaid...* (Corthals, J. (1990 and 2003) in *Celtica* 21, 113-25 and 24, 79-100.) For a slightly different version see Meyer, K. (1914) *Über die älteste irische Dichtung II*, Berlin: Verlag der Königl. Akademie der Wissenschaften, 20. Old Irish. One of the rhymeless poems from the *Book of Leinster*. In line 3 of the Irish *caine* has a range of possible meanings, and *dind* basically means place, as in *dinnseanchas*. However, I am influenced by Meyer's 'gentle' for the first, and I think resting-place is implicit. My 'sojourn' is a direct translation of the Irish *foat* which means to spend the night somewhere (see Thurneysen, 1975: 386). *Temair* is the old Irish name for Tara, the seat of the high kings. I was once invited to read at an international UNESCO poetry festival on the theme of peace. It was striking, and ironic, that readers from several countries confessed that their traditional poetry was warlike, not pacific, praising the feats of great fighters. Ireland is not therefore alone in this, and one has only to go next door to find the great Anglo-Saxon epic *Beowulf*. The war/warrior poems in this book may seem at first sight the most alien to us; if we praise heroes and follow

individual combat now it is likely to be in the (largely) peaceful field of sport. But such poems raise questions for us also, in our own bloody times. I find the warrior poems striking not only in their praise of prowess and bravery but their unflinching description of its consequences: death, suffering, loss and mourning. That said, there seems to have been an acceptance that such conflict was normal; only when it went beyond those norms, as in the killing of an old man who could no longer defend himself (see No 6) did it really shock.

9. *Atomriug indiu...* (Bernard, J. H. and Atkinson, R. (eds) (1898) *The Irish Liber Hymnorum*, Henry Bradshaw Society, London.) See also TP, Vol. 2, 354-58; Greene and O'Connor, 1990; Carey, 2000 and Stifter (2006) section 19.1. 8th century. This is one section of a multi-part poem which is itself one of a collection of hymns put together by a 9th century cleric. A subsequent edition associated it with St. Patrick and it is often known as St. Patrick's breastplate or lorica, but there is no evidence to support this. It is also known in Irish as the *fáeth fiada* (the deer's cry) because of the story that St. Patrick and his followers, on their way to convert the court at Tara, were about to be ambushed by pagan opponents, but prayed to be turned into deer and so escaped. Although the content is clearly Christian, the pattern of repeated invocation sounds pagan, and similar to that in No. 5. Stokes and Strachan in TP translate the opening word *atom-riug* as 'I arise' citing an earlier interpretation of it as *ad-dom-riug* (see p. xl). All the subsequent translations I have seen reject this in favour of 'I gird myself' and I have followed this, although 'bind' might be an alternative. There are slight differences in the wording of all the translations, two of which are worth noting. In line 3, *cumachtae* may have connotations of magical power, rather than simply might, which would rather repeat line 2. In the last line *úathad* usually means a few or a small number, but the DIL gives *i-n-úathad* as alone and I have followed this. Likewise, *sochaidi* can mean a large number, and some have translated this as a crowd or multitude. As in many translations, there is scope for legitimate disagreement. Of early Irish hymns, two have become well known in modern times: this one, through the English version of Cecil Frances Alexander, and *rop tú mo baile* (Be thou my vision) which Murphy dates as 10th/11th century: see his EIL, p. 42.

10. *A rí rind...* (Meyer, K. (1897) *Zeitschrift für celtische Philologie*, 1, 327; Greene and O'Connor, 113). *Leabhar Breac.* One of two separate quatrains in Meyer. The obligation of hospitality is evident in this and some other poems, and characteristic of many traditional societies.

11. *Messe ocus pangur bán...* (TP, Vol. 2, 293-4; EIL). *ca.* 840. A classic example of the seven syllable rhyming *deibide.* This poem was found in a collection of 9th century manuscripts in Austria, and was probably composed by one of the monks who travelled to Europe as clerics or missionaries. It has been widely translated by modern Irish scholars and poets, almost as a rite of passage, including Robin Flower, Frank O'Connor, Eavan Boland, Ruth Lehmann, Paul Muldoon and Seamus Heaney; the last is available online. My version differs markedly from these others, unstitching the prosody of the original while retaining a good deal of the assonance. The monk may have picked up his white Welsh cat Pangur (a 'fuller') on his way to the continent; at any rate, it is one of the most engaging old Irish poems, light and serious at the same time, capturing both the sense of solitariness and companionship; to my mind, unique in the literature in its very personal tone. The constant alternation between 'he' and 'I' is key. Despite its popularity, there has been relatively little scholarly comment on the poem, but see Toner (2009). Drawing on creationist theology, he emphasises that the cat's activities are not simply a metaphor or parallel for those of the scholar, but an example of God-given talents in their own right. Hence he rejects the common translation of *maccdán* as 'childish' or 'childlike' (for the same reason I have translated it as 'his own small pursuits'). Like him, I have avoided the use of the rather limited 'craft' to describe what the scholar and cat do. I also agree that the final *messe* cannot mean 'I' (a clever dual-sense *dúnad*/closure) and in the last line my 'work' is close to his 'service'. However, I have stayed closer to Murphy's paraphrase in EIL in some other ways, and find Toner's analysis a little too solemn to do justice to the serious but playful tone of the original. I suspect that *ferr cach clú* (better than any fame) at the beginning of the second stanza is simply a cheville but I suppose some clerics did acquire celebrity status in their own times.

12. *Bec innocht lúth...* (Meyer, K. (1904) 'Cailte cecinit', *Ériu*, 1, 72-3, text and translation.) Meyer suggests that this poem, from

the *Book of Leinster,* is little older than the twelfth century, thus making it a homage to the much earlier heroic or legendary age of Finn. The poem is put in the mouth of Caoilte, Finn's nephew, who with Oisin, Finn's son, were the only two to survive the final defeat of the Fiana, a tale they supposedly recounted to St. Patrick several centuries later in the *Acallam na Senórach* (see nos 44-46). St. Patrick is again referred to here as 'Adzehead' (see No. 1) and the poem can be seen as a lament for the pagan warrior tradition. In the first line 'heels' have of course no association with running away and refer simply to their physiological importance. Notwithstanding the last line, the poem is written in a high poetic style (*berla filed*) and I have tried to exploit the full range of allusions of words such as *áed* and *baidb* given in the DIL, although I find the line including the second word problematic. Since the last word is the same as the first, the poem is an example of the poetic device of *dúnad* (closure) in the original. For another example of this high style see Carney, J. (1939) 'A poem in Bérla na bFiled', *Éigse,* 1, 85-89.

13. *Adram incoimdid...* Undated. There are two transcriptions of the original in IT, Vol. 3, p. 43, para. 54. See also the translation by Flower (1947). I have maintained the difference between *gel* (bright) and *ban* (white) in the original. The striking thing is that to the poet heaven and earth seem equally real. It is difficult to capture all the connotations of *gel.* At a sensory level, it suggests to me not the brightness of a Mediterranean sun but the glittering vegetation one sometimes sees in Ireland after a sharp shower of rain, creating a sensory clarity that is almost preternaturally real. In early Irish the word had strong religious connotations, a kind of spiritual luminosity which here characterises the angels. It continued to be a strong word in Irish poetry long after this time, for example in the famous vision poem (*aisling*) by Egan O 'Rahilly (1675-1729) which begins '*Gile na gile*' (brightness of brightness) although by then the reference had become transmuted into a vision of a woman representing Ireland. Murphy (1939) distinguishes between three kinds of aisling poem: love/fairy, prophetic and allegorical.

14. *Maith righe Cormaic is Finn...* (Murphy, G. (1933) *Duanaire Finn: the book of the lays of Fionn, Vol. II, 138-40,* London: Irish Texts Society. Although the *Duanaire Finn* is a much later

seventeenth century compilation Murphy dates this poem to the mid-12th century. It is entitled Caoilte's Sword and I have translated only the final stanzas which Murphy suggests might be a prophetic addition. My translation is close to his except in the penultimate stanza where I follow the DIL in translating *sanais* as 'whisper' (he has 'announcement') and in the final stanza where I express the despair in terms of saying rather than doing. The transition from, and relationship between, the older pagan culture and the newer Christian one was a key theme in the early literature. Even later the theme persists, as in a 15th century poem (also in the *Duanaire Finn, No LIII*) which has the repeated lines: *Faoidh cluig do-chúala a nDruim Dheirg/mar a ndéndis in Finn seilg*: I have heard the sound of a bell in Drum Derg/where the Fianna like to hunt…

15. *Uch a lám…* (Meyer, K. (1899) *Zeitschrift für celtische Philologie*, 2, 225). (NB this poem does not appear in the archive.org table of contents but is in the URL text). Meyer's note on the source (H.3.18, p. 478 marg. inf.) suggests that this is a gloss on an early manuscript, but does not give a date. The last line (*ad benn lom cuail cnám*) is so compact that I could not work in *benn*.

16. *In bith trúag i taam…* (Stokes, W. (1905) *Félire Óengusso Céli Dé: the Martyrology of Oengus the Culdee*. London: Henry Bradshaw Society; see also Greene and O'Connor, pp. 61-5; Carey, 2000.) About 800. Prologue lines 157-173, 209-212, 237-240. The *Felire Oengusso* is a calendar of saints, a kind of aide-memoire listing those associated with each day of the year, but it is topped and tailed by a much more interesting Prologue and Epilogue. The stanzas here are selected from the first, and celebrate the triumph of Christianity over paganism in Ireland. The first line has the first occurrence I have come across of the word *trúag* (sorry). It was to become a familiar word in Irish poetry over the ages and is still used in quite ordinary contexts. The cheville *delm sochla* (a thunderous message) in the second stanza is difficult to translate and this is my best shot. Greene and O'Connor tone down the reference to Rome (*rúama*) to 'sanctuary' (the dictionary also gives 'monastery') but I have given the hyperbole full volume. The reference to spear-points in the last stanza here suggests that the triumph involved force as well as spiritual power, and I have tried to catch the biblical echo in the last line. It is possible that the author of

this poem also had a hand in the slightly later Martyrology of Tallaght. For the references to both poems see the van Hamel or CELT websites. The *Ceili Dé* (companions of God, anglicised as Culdee) was a religious movement which began around 800 and later spread beyond Ireland. There is a substantial literature about it. It might seem strange to us that such a movement was felt to be needed, but we have to remember that by then it was over 300 years since Patrick's mission, and over 200 since the death of Columba.

17. *Dom-farcai fidbaide fál...* (TP, Vol. 2, 290; EIL). Early 9th c. This well-known little poem has given rise to a great deal of comment. To begin with, the phrase *hi mbrot glass* (in a grey mantle) is interesting in that *brot* is derived from the Latin word for cloak or mantle (Kuno Meyer provides lists of loanwords from various languages in early Irish in volumes 11, 12 and 13 of the *Revue Celtique*). And whereas *glass* covered various colours then (see Note 80) it means only green in Modern Irish. Mantle in English means among other things the back feathers of a bird, but here it is 'in', implying wearing, rather than 'with'. (Greene and O'Connor assume the green bush is the mantle.) In the same line, *dingnaib* is usually translated as 'the top of' but the DIL also gives 'eminence', 'fort' or 'stronghold' in other contexts: which raises the question of what the context of this poem really is. Although it reads like a 'nature' poem, there are several human allusions: the blackbird composes poetic odes, the cuckoo makes a speech and wears a cloak. In line 3 (*huas mo lebrán ind línech*) Ó Corráin (1989, see note 29) suggests that *lebrán* means 'a gathering' but the DIL after 'little book' gives as its second meaning a copy or transcript, quoting the phrase *re gach lebar a lebrán*: to each book its copy which was used in the dispute over Columba's copy (see No 80). Both Thurneysen (1975, p. 298) and Stifter (2006, p. 50) note the unusual syntax of this line; I have reproduced this exactly ('above my book   the lined one') since I think it gives a particular intimacy and immediacy to the situation. I have translated *dingnaib doss* as 'from the top of a bush-fort' (cf Murphy's 'fortresses') on the grounds that even if the latter was not the primary sense, people then would have picked up the secondary resonance. The last line in the original and second last in my translation are problematic. The TP text reads

debrath nomchoimmdiu coíma and is translated as 'may the Lord protect me from doom'. However the DIL comments that this translation is impossible. *Debrath* was an exclamation or asseveration often used by St. Patrick, which refers to the day of judgement; the nearest English equivalent might be 'God save us'. However Murphy introduces an exclamation mark after it, separating it from the rest of the line, which he annotates as 'the Lord befriends me'. On the other hand Stifter (p. 264) has 'may God be kind to me'. I have followed Murphy since the statement, rather than plea, seems to fit better with the final line. Although this poem refers to the natural world, the above analysis thus shows that it is actually quite literary and far from being some spontaneous effusion. Different scholars have reacted to it in different ways. Ó Corráin describes it as professional, languid and polished. Toner (2009) sees it as genuinely spiritual, placing it in the context of creation theology, which stresses the bounty of the Creator of the natural world, a world which here surrounds and enfolds the writer in God's goodness; whereas Ó Corráin describes it as egotistical, noting that there is a personal reference in every line but one. One scholar has however taken an altogether different tack. Ford (1999) points out that the poem occurs as a gloss on two pages of a Latin grammar which deal with the position of pronouns in Latin. He argues that the teacher might well have used Irish pronouns as a comparison, and notes that this particular poem contains five examples of Irish infixed pronouns (which do not occur in Latin). The poem would thus take on the role of, and was perhaps composed as, a teaching aid. This suggestion is endorsed by Melia (2005) who while remarking on the 'figures of enclosure' in the poem states 'The poem was where it was found in the manuscript as an illustration of the main text' (p. 286). The actual gloss can now be viewed online (see the original at the end of this book). Each of the two stanzas as they appear in Murphy's EIL is written as a single long line along the bottom margin of the double column text on pages 203/204 (the page numbers can be faintly read at the top). There is a mid-line dot at the end of each couplet (after *cél* and *doss*) and two dots and a comma after *innanén* at the end of the first page, suggesting that the writer already knew what was to follow. Otherwise there is no punctuation; none of the subsequent printings I have seen, including that of the St. Gall Priscian project at NUI Galway (StGallPriscian.ie), reproduces exactly the original layout, most inserting mid-line dots as they appear in TP. On p. 203 the word *fidbaide* has been omitted from the gloss and then inserted below the line with what look like insertion marks. On p. 204, the *a* in *coíma* is omitted and added below the line. Was the poem composed at that point or remembered or copied from another, earlier source? As Murphy notes, the poem is in regular metre (*rannaigecht*) and has both end- and internal rhymes; indeed it is very well constructed and could not simply have been dashed off. A line reading *dom-farcai fál* would have been rhythmically impossible; *fidbaide* is essential to both metre and sense; likewise the 'a' in *cóima*. Although we cannot know, these omissions/insertions suggest to me that the poem was copied or transcribed, a little faultily, from memory, not composed by the glossator, and its grammatical application, if such there was, was purely incidental. I do not therefore agree with Ford's contention that the poem's manuscript context is essential to its understanding; Toner disagrees also and Clancy (2014: 11) likewise engages in 'a cautious act of reclamation', revising the revisionists. While recognizing the literary and technical aspects of this and other nature poems, he re-affirms their authentic, empirical basis, pointing out how their subjectivity is embodied in various persona, here the monk/scribe.

18. *Ili insi Mod...* (BL, 9, No 12). Undated. Kuno Meyer (1910) published a long list of poems on the O'Donnells in *Ériu*, 4, 183-90. Many of these are Middle Irish or later and although this poem is not itemised, it may thus belong to that period. (The UCC CELT archive also contains 25 poems (again not including this one) on the O'Donnells, 1200-1600, edited by J. Fraser and J.G. O'Keefe, in *Irish Texts, Fasc.II*; nor is it cited in the article by Ó Cléirigh on a poem book of the O'Donnells in *Éigse* 1, 1939). The names in the poem are archaic, but it is difficult to know if this signals real age or poetic archaism; on balance I have decided to include it. The mountain in the poem is called *Cruachan Aigli*. I have used the modern name Croagh Patrick although it probably had no association with St. Patrick then. In his gloss, Meyer notes that Clew Bay (*Mod*

in the original) is supposed to have 365 islands. The Irish is neat, each line beginning with *'ili'* (many) but finishing off with *'lia'* (more than). A typical if amusing example of bardic hyperbole. The genre is explored in Mac Cana, 1988; Mac Cana, 2004; and Breatnach, 2006.

19. *Mac Rig Múaide...* (BL, 69, No. 161). Undated. This is Moy in Co. Mayo, not Tyrone. The first line reads literally 'the son of the king of Moy'; perhaps the word 'prince' did not become established in the language until later, through Norman influence. The last line is obscure but does mention reeds.

20. *Mo theora ucse...* (Meyer, K. (1910) *Zeitschrift für celtische Philologie*, 7, 309-10, text only; (1912) 'Four religious poems', *Ériu,* 6, 112-16, text and translation.) Old Irish, undated. The last of the set of four. The formulaic, almost legal, side of Celtic piety comes out here. It may well seem somewhat naïve to us now, and perhaps also reflects the earlier pattern of pagan wishes and curses, but was nonetheless genuine. As noted above, some early Irish verse is quite formulaic, and this may represent a blend of both traditions, pre-Christian and Christian. Indeed, one might argue that formalism also has its place in modern Irish writing, notably in Joyce's *Ulysses* and *Finnegans Wake*, and that 'form' generally is a fruitful line of analysis in Irish literature. However, even in this rather formulaic poem, the ear for language is apparent in lines such as *nímraib náma nímraib ní.* The third last line may serve as an example of the kinds of problems that these poems can throw up. It reads *ní dern séithar cen fochraich fiad Chríst in domain chía,* which Meyer translates as 'may I do no work without reward before the Christ of this world'. Reward is probably right for *fochraich,* although given the vagaries of old Irish spelling, the word is also close to *fochrach* meaning 'hireling' which would give us the interesting but probably erroneous 'may I do no work except as a hireling of Christ'. *Fiad* means 'in the eyes of' or 'in the presence of' and carries a sense of judgement. Meyer's translation of *Chríst in domain chía* as 'Christ of this world' does not seem quite right. The DIL cites no other instance of this phrase, so we have no other context to refer to. It is possible that it was a formulaic religious expression now lost, meaning Christ who came to or saved this world, but I think that it probably refers back to the writer

here, since it is in the genitive case, although the syntax would be unusual.

21. *Clocán binn...* (IT, Vol. 3, p. 16, no. 40; EIL; Greene and O'Connor, 113). 9th c. Irish bells were struck, not rung with a clapper. Women were clearly a temptation for the monks, and there is more than a hint of misogyny running through the old Irish Triads, a collection of commonly agreed statements about things usually in threes (translated by Kuno Meyer and now available online).

22. *Scél lem dúib...* (The oldest source appears to be Best R. I. and Bergin, O., (1929) *Lebor na Huidre: book of the dun cow.* Royal Irish Academy, Dublin, p.30; see also *Revue Celtique,* 20, 258-59, 1899; KM; EIL). 9th or 10th c. I have stayed with these texts although one scholar has argued that S1c,d should be the other way round: see Bisagni, J. (2008) ' Scél lem dúib: an emendation,' *Studia Celtica,* 42, 166-71. This famous poem forms part of the Finn cycle, although as noted earlier such placing could have been subsequent; I sense it is free-standing. It has been translated frequently and is very condensed, with lines of just three or four syllables (see the original at the end of the book). The belling of the stag indicates that this was the autumnal rutting season, but since the word *dordaid* is not onomatopoeic, and can refer to a variety of sounds, I have preferred 'gives voice'. After some agonising, I decided to use 'wild goose' despite the subsequent unwanted historical associations, but rejected Whitley Stokes' embellishment of the last line in RC: 'sad is my tale'. Perhaps more than any other, this poem demonstrates the extraordinary economy of some early Irish poetry, a feature which is of course very difficult to bring across in translation: I have had to employ four or five syllables per line. The person of the poet is present, but only in the implied reaction to oncoming winter; personal expression is confined to the first and last lines, and this I think makes the poem all the more telling. Indeed, like a later poem, this one can be seen as curiously modern in its 'objectivism': the reduction, even excision, of any overt subjective element. For a pedagogical breakdown of the grammar of this and some other poems see the relevant University of Texas website (www.utexas.edu/cola/centers/irc...). I have chosen the first line as my book title since I think the richness of this early Irish poetry will be news to many.

23. *Ind ráith i comair in dairfedo...* (BL; EIL, p. xvi; MIL, p. x). Undated. The fort refers to the one at Rathangan, Co. Offaly. Names, both of people and places, feature a good deal in old Irish poetry, the first often for bardic or historical reasons, the second evincing the love of place or locality and the people and events associated with them. It is interesting to ask how people in those days constructed their sense of time or historicity. The need to do so helps explain the emphasis on genealogy, and many poems trace back the generations in that way. Another means would have been, as in this poem, to reflect on old buildings, as physical presences or remains from the past. In some cases, as with standing-stones or tombs, their origins would have been as mysterious to people in the 8th century as to us now.

24. *Ach a luin is buide duit...* (BL; MIL, pp. 206-7). This poem is in the margins of the *Leabhar Breac* (Speckled Book) which was compiled in 1408-11 but which contains a great variety of materials spanning many centuries. The text is unusual both in the number of marginalia there are and the care with which they have been written: as the introduction to the RIA digital version states: 'The early anonymous marginalia are as carefully written as the work itself, and it is difficult at times to distinguish between these early hands and the main scribe (see ISOS Irish Scripts on Screen: Collections: Royal Irish Academy). Ó Concheanainn (1973) has dated some of the marginalia which refer to contemporaneous events but notes that this and other poems cannot be dated. While it is thus likely that they are by the scribe, it is possible they come from other, earlier sources. Carney translates *síthamail* in the last line as 'fairylike' from the root *síd* meaning fairy. We would thus have an interesting mix of pagan and Christian in the same poem. However, the DIL does not give *síthamail* in this sense but as meaning 'peaceful' (the root *síd* also means peace). I have therefore reluctantly concluded that 'peaceful' is more likely to be right and have followed Meyer and Jackson in this. However, it has been argued that the two meanings of peace and otherworld were originally linked: see Ó Catharsaigh (1977-8). Blackbirds were a favourite subject in early Irish poetry, including in some poems not translated here, and continued to be so: there is a fine 17th century poem beginning *'Binn sin, a luin Doire an Chairn:'* Beautiful –

blackbird of Doire an Chairn'; see Ó Tuama and Kinsella (1981: 40). (The blackbird was also Samuel Beckett's favourite bird.) This little poem also raises a more general issue. Early Irish poetry has in the past been prized for, among other things, its 'nature' lyrics and it is true that this was a significant, although not major, strand in the literature, exemplified by this and several other poems in this book. One might also point to the many pictures of animals, birds and fish in the *Book of Durrow* and *Book of Kells*; some of these are symbolic, but many are not. However, we need to be careful. The early Anglophone, French and German Celtic scholars brought from their own languages powerful 19th century concepts of nature/*la nature/Natur*. In recent times, these have been reinforced (if also modified) by the environmental movement and a consciousness of 'earth' as our home. This comes close to essentialising Nature. However, different cultures 'construct' or see the natural world in different ways and we cannot assume that early Irish culture saw it in the way we do. The DIL gives *aicned* for 'nature' but this is in the philosophical sense of the nature or essence of something. I cannot find any word that directly corresponds to our modern sense of 'the natural world'. The nearest is perhaps *dúil* (as in *a De dúilig*) which means creation. However, this is all-encompassing and includes the human. Indeed, I doubt very much whether 'nature' was conceived of in an independent or essential way, but rather as a manifestation of God's entire creation. Perhaps we should draw a distinction between 'nature' and 'the natural world'. Early Irish poetry patently refers to the latter sometimes; but that does not mean that it carries all the associations we have of the former. For a discussion, see Sims-Williams (1996).

25. *Fuitt co bráth...* (KM, no 4; MIL, pp. 22-25). Probably 9th c. On the construction of this and other seasonal poems see Note 79. The Irish preamble in KM identifies Cuilt as being on Slieve Gullion, Co. Armagh, where there are a court tomb and mythological associations with Finn. The word *cuilt* means a corner or nook as in the common prefix *cuil* (cf. Coleraine, the corner with the small fort). There are no parentheses in the original but following Carney I have introduced them to help overcome the disjunction of the seventh line, which nevertheless forms part of the general conceit of magni-fication, although it might refer empirically to the visual

illusion created by light on snow. The phrase *caill cach móin*, literally 'a wood each bog' cannot refer to trees which don't grow in bogs or moorland, so I have assumed relates to the difficulty of passage: in those days woods were dense, tangled and sometimes dangerous places. In the final stanza Meyer translates *iar ngleo glicc* as 'after a sharp struggle' and Carney as 'encircling with cunning' but *gleo* means fighting so I think 'ambushing' is justified here. It is a nice conceit in relation to a standing-stone.

26. *Fiu mór do maith Máel Fábaill...* (BL, p. 11, no. 17). Date uncertain. This poem was almost certainly written by a woman admirer. I have translated *óenri*, literally 'one (and only) king' as 'peerless'. There are undertones of competition and jealousy.

27. *Is mebul dom imrádud...* (Robert Atkinson, *The Passions and the Homilies from Leabhar Breac*, Royal Irish Academy, Dublin, 1887: 262; Meyer, K. (1907) 'A religious poem', *Ériu*, 3: 14; EIL). 10th c. There is also a lively version in O'Connor (1959). The 7/5/7/5 stanza gives the Irish a pacey rhythm. In stanza three the word *chathracha* is usually translated as 'cities' although the DIL does also give 'settlements'. This may be one of the many flights of fancy in the poem, since there were no cities in Ireland at that time; perhaps the writer was thinking of Rome or Paris. Stanza four is incomplete in the original. In the final stanza Meyer glosses *cétchummaid* as 'in his first company' but I have taken it to mean Christ and his original disciples rather than Murphy's 'perfect companionship'. Although the lines may refer to Christ only, I find it hard to believe that the writer would have even contemplated the possibility that Christ himself was inconstant, so have made it a composite reference. At this point it may be appropriate to raise the question: how far do these spiritual poems give us an insight into the religion of the times? Two cautions immediately suggest themselves: first we are talking about a time-span of some six centuries, during which there was a good deal of change, and secondly the small set of poems here forms only a minute sample of the large corpus of religious writing, mainly prose, of the period. There is an extensive scholarly literature on the development of Christianity in Ireland which addresses various issues. In what ways did the new religion accommodate, assimilate, displace or suppress the existing pagan belief system? We know that

some pagan sites, such as wells, became Christianised and that some important pagan dates came to coincide with Christian ones, such as the birth of St. Brigid; that there was some mismatch between existing civil laws and Christian ones, for example in relation to marriage and divorce; that the spread of the new religion was geographically uneven; and that pagan belief seemed to decline sharply in the wake of some natural disasters (plague, famine) in the 6th century. What was the relationship between the 'insular' church in Ireland and Britain and the authority of Rome? Some writers emphasise the differences, sometimes in support of a notional 'Celtic' Christianity, others largely discount them. How did the diocesan structure put in place by Patrick relate to the monasteries, which became power-houses of the new faith? How real or idealized was the hermetic model, which features in several poems? Most monks would have lived in monastic communities, but as Toner (2009) points out, some left them temporarily to adopt a solitary life. My own view is that the poems here give us glimpses, flashes of that world but that it would be hazardous to try to generalise much from them.

28. *Noísi do rónad a fert... (Longes mac n-Uislenn: the exile of the sons of Uisliu).* One of the prefatory stories to the *Tain* in the *Book of Leinster.* The latter is 12th century but the story may be much older. Sources: IT, Vol. 1, pp. 59-92, translated stanzas pp. 78-9, German commentary; revised CELT edition of Vernam Hull's 1949 edition (for the various editions and translations see the van Hamel website); Thomas Kinsella's translation of *The Tain* (1969). See also Buttimer (1994-5) who focusses on the progression of the prose narrative and regards the verse as a textual intrusion: another take on the prose/verse relationship flagged up in the contextual notes; see also Mac Cana (1997) and Note 42. The verse is irregular. The story of Deirdre is one of the best known in all Irish literature and has inspired a number of modern versions. The king of Ulster is dining with his chief musician when the baby whom the latter's wife is carrying screams in her womb. A seer foretells that the baby will be a girl, who will grow up to be a beautiful *femme fatale* who will cause many deaths. The king decides to have her reared in seclusion until she is ready to marry him, but she meets a fine young warrior, Naoise and elopes with

him and his two brothers. They elude the king for some years but are tricked into returning and the three brothers are killed. The king takes Deirdre as his wife but she is recalcitrant. After a year he asks her whom she hates most and she names him and Naoise's killer. He then orders her to go and live with the latter for a year. On the way, she jumps out of the chariot and her head is dashed against a stone. Murphy (EIL, pp. xvii-xviii) considered this text to be so corrupt as to be unworkable and there are serious uncertainties, in particular with the lines *inmain berthán áilli blai/tuchtach duine cid dind-blai.* I take the first line to refer to Naoise's hair, whereas Kinsella thinks it is about his fleece jacket; and I have omitted the second which I cannot make sense of. Because of such difficulties, I have gone for a freer version, working both forwards and back from stanza 8 in Deirdre's first poem, and incorporating some of the prose at the end as well; purists may wish to compare this with the sources above. I see the poem not only as a love-lament but as an evocation of brotherhood. There is no mention of a fatal draught in the original story, so the sense is metaphorical. For a discussion of the perception of Deirdre's behaviour as a woman in the context of the times, see Bitel (1996: 51-2). Clancy (2005: 179) points out that Deirdre's strength of character emerges well in a story in which both king and court come out badly, and justice is not seen to be done.

29. *Ar currucán cumraide...* (BL, 70, no. 163). Included in Dillon (1994: 156). No date given. To me, this poem suggests a hermit living on a lake shore or perhaps island, although Ó Corráin (1989) has questioned the whole idea of 'hermit poems'. As Ó Corráin explains, some earlier scholars such as Meyer, Flower and Hughes, influenced by notions of Celtic naturalism, saw these poems as the spontaneous effusions of hermits, separated from people but close to nature, and perhaps associated with the Anchoritic movement of the 8th/9th centuries. He argues that in fact they were probably written by members or even leaders of monastic communities, expressing an eremitic ideal, and that their construction is artful and even mannered. Ó Corráin's chapter brought about a marked shift in the scholarly literature in the way these poems are viewed, though the popular perception of them has probably not changed much. Several points can be made. First Ó

Corráin states (p. 252) that 'Unfortunately, Columcille has left us hardly any of his reflections on nature, and the pagan Irish none at all'. The latter is strictly true of pre-Christian poems, but there are a number of 'nature' poems written during the Christian era which are not at all Christian in reference or tone, including 25, 36, 44, 50, 57 and 79 in this collection. Secondly, Ó Corráin's list of 14 Christian 'nature' poems is incomplete and does not include 78 or this one. Here, the poet's little house (or cell?) is kept *glan*, a strong Irish word, meaning clean, pure, tidy, perhaps because that is holy. The crane is his only companion; *dóer* here surely cannot mean 'servant' as Meyer has it but base or low-born, because it is only a bird. (A pet crane is also mentioned in *The Vision of Mac Conglinne*.) After becoming extinct in Ireland about 300 years ago, cranes have been sighted recently again flying over the country and this has reawakened interest in references to them in the past. It seems they were prized as pets and perhaps also had druidical significance. It is possible, though not certain, that some place names incorporating *cor* referred originally to them.) I think Ó Corráin is right in seeing the Christian nature poems as forming a genre, expressing an ideal. It is possible that some of them were written by monks who had gone off to live alone for a while, apparently a quite common practice; life in the monastery, with its inescapable proximities and no doubt tensions, must have been a real trial at times, and the idea of the holy hermit, which originated in early Christianity in the Middle East, must have held a powerful attraction for both genuine and pragmatic reasons; at least for a while. However, I think Ó Corráin is too ready to write off the real substance of the poems; the fact that something is a genre or convention does not mean that it cannot contain real substance or feeling; that is a peculiarly modern prejudice, based on our contemporary notions of 'authenticity' or 'originality'. The bulk of art of all kinds in the past has been 'conventional'.

30. *Día mba trebthach...* (Meyer, K. (1905) *Ériu*, 2, 172.) Undated. The obscurity of some of the diction means I have had to rely more on Meyer than I would like. This rather sententious little poem nevertheless gives a good sense of how religious faith was expected to translate into moral and social terms. Charles-Edwards (2000: 137) defines *trebar* as 'a good farmer and head

of household', a valued status among commoners. As noted earlier, chevilles or interjections can be difficult to translate, and here I have rendered *aslondath ní dis*, which Meyer gives as 'no trifling saying' as 'think of that'. What strikes me about this line is the emphasis on the figure of Christ, as a person who might arrive at one's door; the underlying mystery of the incarnation. More broadly, I sense that figures were important in the culture, in a way that I find difficult to put my finger on; but the figures of Finn or Cú Chulainn were emblematic or iconic in the pagan world and the same seems to have been true of the figures of the Christian saints, such as Patrick, Brigit and Columcille. I wonder if the culture was one of embodiment rather than abstraction; if ideas such as nobility, bravery, virtue or holiness typically found form in, or were represented by, human figures. However, we must be careful not to imply an incapacity to abstract or conceptualise, which the respect for 'wisdom' in pagan times or 'learning' in the Christian era would rebut. Returning to this poem, it must also have been the pious practice to give first fruits (*prímedach*) to a local religious community. Meyer could not make sense of the line *sech ní maithe ní máide*: the DIL gives 'not only do not fail to give it but do not boast of it' (on *maidem* see Thurneysen 1975: 42). Clancy (1991: online page 191-92) likewise omits it. Thurneysen (1975: 550) cites the construction *sech ni... ni* as an antithetical form of neither/nor and here it has the run of a stock phrase. I suspect therefore that *maithe* is the opposite of *maíde*, perhaps derived from *maeithe* which can mean mildness or weakness.

31. *Di chíanab...* Ó Cuiv, B. (1948) 'A quatrain from "Liadain and Curithir", *Éigse* V (4), 229-230. This comes from an old, prosimetric, tragic love story. The poetess Liadain is making a tour through Connaught when she meets the poet Curithir who throws a party for her and then asks her to marry him ('a son of ours would be famous'). She demurs, not wishing to interrupt her journey, but says that if he travels afterwards to her house in Munster she will agree. By the time he does so, she has taken the veil. The couple place themselves in the hands of a priest who orders them to spend a night together but with a young scholar lying between them. In the morning, the priest orders the boy on pain of death to tell the truth, whereas

Curithir tells him on pain of death not to. Curithir is banished to another parish, where he utters these lines (which are in a different metre from the other stanzas). When Liadain seeks him out, he hears that she is coming and goes abroad; she dies of grief, having uttered a lament. For the various editions and translations see the van Hamel site. For a discussion of the feminine aspect see Larson (2005).

32. *Teicht do Róim...* (TP, Vol. 2, 396). The text is a three-line gloss along the bottom margin of p. 45 of the *Codex Boernerianus*, a collection of Pauline epistles in Greek with Latin translation above the line, found in a Swiss monastery and dated 850-900, which can now be viewed online. *INrí* is written thus. The end of what is nowadays printed as the first stanza overruns onto the second line of the gloss, with a line guiding the eye down. The second stanza is discussed by Clancy (1991, online page 32) in terms of the relationship between madness and sin. The syntax of the second stanza is also discussed in passing by Uhlich (2006) who sees the fourth line as consequential upon the first and second: 'great is the folly... since going to death is certain/that it should be under the displeasure of Mary's Son'. 'Under the displeasure' literally translates *fo étóil* but it is not English. And while 'displeasure' nicely carries on the royal conceit of the first stanza the word is the opposite of *toll* which means will or wish and thus has a much stronger sense of rejection. (The DIL definition of *étol* simply quotes this line and is thus circular.) And while *fo* suggests 'being subject to' S2a, b imply choice. The meaning of the poem is clear enough, but the tone is difficult to calibrate: the neat, ironic formula of the first stanza contrasts with the wordy vehemence of the second, making one wonder if the two really belong together.

33. *M'aenarán dam isa sliab...* (Carney, J. (1940) 'M'aenarán dam isa sliab', *Éigse*, 2(2), 107-13). There are two distinct versions of this poem, each of which has two variants. I have followed Carney's text which combines the two variants of what is probably the older version from a detached page (and there were quite a few) of the *Book of Leinster*. There are only three stanzas which are at all common to the two versions. The later one, from the *Yellow Book of Lecan* (which was compiled about 1400) was edited and translated by John O'Donovan (1846) *The Miscellany of the Irish Archaeological Society*, 1, 1-15 and

edited by Kuno Meyer (1910) *ZCP*, VII, 302. The YBL version contrasts Christian trust in God with pagan reliance on 'superstition': 'It is not with the *sreod* our destiny is/nor with the bird on the top of the twig/nor with the trunk of a knotty tree/nor with a *sordan* hand in hand/better is He in whom we trust/The Father, the One, and the Son'. Carney thinks that this later version was reconstructed to place the life of Columcille in the context of the struggle to overcome pagan beliefs, and the poem climaxes with 'My Druid is Christ, the Son of God'. The composition is technically poorer, but the existence of now incomprehensible pagan references such as *sreod* raises an interesting question: could this version have drawn also on a quite different, older manuscript, or did the YBL poet make up these words to give a sense of authenticity? Carney's version makes no overt reference to paganism and appears to be wholly about the Christian notion of predestination. Any religion which posits an omniscient, omnipotent God is at least open to this idea, and associated fatalism, which of course have to be reconciled with the concepts of free will and moral responsibility. However, the idea that one's place of death (the *fód* 'sod') was pre-ordained was a pre-Christian, pagan Irish one, and one wonders how far the poem is also imbued with such older beliefs. Carney comments on this in his introduction in MIL, which contains a looser verse translation, and on the Christian idea that sneezing involved the expelling of a devil, prompting the response we still sometimes make: 'bless you'. Several other points are worth noting. Old Irish has a distinct set of terms for counting people rather than things, hence *m'aen ʒrán*. In S1c I have translated *ina mend* as 'assuredly' following the DIL entry of 'clear' or 'evident' rather than Carney's 'pitfalls'.The army of 'three thousand' appears here again. The YBL version reads this as *tri fichit cét* (3 x 20 x 100) and although this may simply be a discrepancy, it is repeated in a 16th century life of the saint (Manus O'Donnell's *Betha Colaim Chille*, section 171) which places the poem in the context of the conflict about the copied book and has him going on alone to avoid the king's soldiers. In S2c, *báis brais* may be there mainly for the alliteration, and could mean various things (brash? boastful? mighty?) as well as 'violent' death. In stanza 5, I have translated *duinén* literally as 'little person', the diminutive '*én*' connoting condescension; a modern equivalent might be 'nonentity'. In the final stanza I have rendered the striking phrase *i n uathaibh báis báin* as 'the horror   the blanch of death' but the Irish is if anything more powerful. As Carney's notes indicate, there are a number of uncertainties in this text and my translation is necessarily tentative in places.

34. *Ferrdi in liath a Muig Mell...* (Carey, J. (1996) 'A posthumous quatrain', *Éigse* XXIX, 172-74.) From *Leabhar Breac*. Headed *Anima post mortem*, this single quatrain refers to the standard practice of praying for souls in purgatory, with a certain wry humour. Carey notes that the phrase *mag mell* is usually applied to the otherworld paradise, rather than Christian heaven.

35. *A Bé find in rega lim...* (Windisch, E. (1880) *Irische Texte mit Wörterbuch, Vol. IV: Tochmarc Etáine*, Leipzig: Hirzel, pp. 132-3. No later than 1100. See also the translations by O'Faoláin (1938: 89), Murphy (1956: 104-7) and Lehmann (1982: 65-66). This poem forms part of the mythological 'Wooing of Etain' which derives from several different sources and about which there is a considerable scholarly literature. In the poem, Queen Etain's previously deceased husband-king has returned from the otherworld to try to persuade her to go back there with him, hence the reference to the crown at the end. I have radically re-ordered the lines of this very disjunctive poem which nevertheless in the original rhymes all four lines of the final stanza. I have translated *corcur* in the Irish stanza 3 as 'purple' but as noted in the Arran poem it can also mean red; here I think the reference is to heather (as in Yeats' *Inisfree*). As Murphy explains in an extended note, the young not dying before the old was a reference to Christian descriptions of a happy society. In my first stanza and the final Irish, most people have translated *muc úr* as 'fresh (i.e. unsalted) pork'. However, *úr* can also mean fleshy, so I have preferred 'succulent'. Also in the final Irish stanza, most previous translators have treated *tind* as a variant of *tend* (strong, vigorous) but the DIL gives *tind* separately as 'bright, shining'. In the last line I have gone for 'magical' partly because I think it captures the true sense of the poem, and also because the other options of 'wonderful' or 'marvellous' have become weak in English. The poem exhibits an interesting mixture of pagan and Christian beliefs. Belief

in the 'otherworld' was a feature of early (and not so early!) Irish culture and this poem provides just one example of its importance. The reference to Adam however suggests an orthodox Augustinian view of original sin rather than the Pelagian heresy which some have suggested had an influence on early insular Christianity.

36. *Fégaid úaib...* (IT, Vol. 3, p. 38, no 24; BL; MIL; Greene and O'Connor). Undated. I cannot better Carney's 'teeming with sea-life'. Like other short poems, this one is printed in two lines with in-line spaces in Meyer's *Bruchstücke*.

37. *Dúthracar a maic Dé bí...* (Meyer, K. (1904) 'Comad Machin Leith annso', *Ériu*, 1, 38-40; EIL.) 9th or 10th c. Also translated by Jackson and Greene and O'Connor. Somewhat irregular 7/5/7/5 stanzas; the pace is quite stately and I have perhaps unconsciously used some iambic pentameters to capture this. I find this poem more than a little contrived (it was written by a scribe and ascribed to St. Manchin, thus perhaps idealised) but it has some fine lines. The problem of the colour of *glas* (green? grey? blue?) occurs again in the first line of stanza 2 and is exacerbated by *tre* (very); I have implied the last in my line 7. In stanza 6 of the original, I have translated the line *cuibdi fri cach les* as 'suitable in every respect' (Meyer has 'fit for every need', Murphy 'to suit every need' and Stifter (p. 353) 'harmonious in every matter'). However the line could perhaps refer to the surrounding arithmetic permutations and be translated as 'whichever way you want': even in serious poems there is sometimes an element of play. In stanza 9 the line *fri deithidin cuirp* has been variously translated as 'for the care of the body' (Meyer and others) and 'for tending the body' (Murphy). However, I think the sense here is simply of everyday bodily needs i.e. a dormitory/refectory, rather than the physical asceticism found in other poems, and have added 'eating   sleeping' to make this clear. There is some disagreement about the fish at the end: Meyer has a comma separating *bradain, breca* and translates 'salmon, trout' whereas Murphy has excised it, giving him 'speckled salmon'. I think the little stream (*sruthán*) mentioned earlier would have contained salmon-trout rather than salmon.

38. *Críde hé...* (BL; MIL, p. 28; Greene and O'Connor, p. 112). 9th or 10th c. In his *Bruchstücke* Meyer glosses the acorn/oak line as

ein Nuss des Eichenwaldes. Another poem by a woman; it could refer to a young boy or young man. I suspect the latter.

39. *M'airiuclán hi Túaim Inbir* (TP, Vol. 2, 394; EIL; Greene and O'Connor). 11th c. Murphy has an extended note on this; see also Carney (1950) and Jackson (1953). This poem has been the subject of a good deal of debate and been interpreted in two different ways. The first is as a Christian hermit poem, perhaps spoken by St. Moling (sometimes written Mo Ling). In support of this one may adduce the reference to an oratory (an outdoor place of prayer), the mention of Gobbán as a famous builder of churches and monasteries and the subsequent and perhaps distinct reference to God as creator of the heavens (sun, moon and stars). Opinions differ as to whether Gobban was real or mythical, but he certainly features in an Irish biography of St. Moling, translated by Whitley Stokes. On the other hand, an early manuscript source treats the poem as part of the *Suibhne Geilt* (Mad/Wild/Crazy Sweeney) cycle (O'Keeffe, 1931). Like Sweeney, the poet lives in the tree-tops (the epigraph *barr edin*) like a bird and is also at risk from spear-points, being pursued as an outcast, which Moling was not. It is possible that the text is a fusion of the two stories. In line 3, referring to the stars, Jackson (p. 72) translates *a réir* as 'as ordained' but Stokes and Strachan in TP have 'last night'. In the latter, the Irish is printed as one word, *aréir*, and such differences in spacing add to the widespread difficulties of variation in spelling in old Irish, comprehensively recorded in the DIL. Carney (1955: 135) argues that Gobban refers not to the quasi-historical figure but is a common noun meaning 'artisan' and that the artisan here is God. Logically, it should not thus be capitalised, but coming at the beginning of a stanza it is in all the editions I have seen (the original is in St. Paul's monastery in Carinthia, Austria). Murphy disagrees but one has to consider the poem as a whole, which establishes a profound difference between the human world (a large house full of people, spear-points, fence) and the natural, God-given world of the tree-tops. The human figure of Gobban does not fit this scheme, indeed obtrudes. I have therefore followed Carney and translated *gobbán* by the 17th century religious phrase, Great Artificer, used by others, including James Joyce, subsequently. Thurneysen (1975: 232) cites the second last line '*soilsidir bid hi lubgurt*' ('as light as a garden') as an example of the equative adjectival form; later

he suggests that it might mean 'as bright as being in a garden' (Thurneysen, 1975: 489). Among the Indo-European languages this construction is unique to the insular Celtic ones, but occurs in some ancient Middle Eastern languages, perhaps supporting the idea of a non-Indo-European substratum. The Sweeney poems form a powerful sequence on the theme of the outcast who goes mad. It has been translated by, among others, Seamus Heaney and Trevor Joyce. While its story of transgression, curse, banishment and eventual retribution is very much of its time, it has I think a powerful modern appeal in the theme of alienation from the social world and (temporary) refuge in the natural one.

40. *Gaib do chuil isin charcair...* (TP, Vol. 2, 290). Probably 840-850. One of the poetic glosses in the St. Gall Priscian, which appears to bear no relationship to the Latin grammar text at that point. The poem forms a single long line in the top margin of the page with a single dot after *colcaid*. There are no emendations. We can only guess at the circumstances behind this bitter little poem. Was the glossator in some kind of trouble? The handwriting in the St. Gall manuscript suggests there were at least two glossators, although given the immense size of the task (the double column text runs to nearly 250 pages) that is not surprising. The third line is obscure although *amail* means fool or simpleton and *bachal* a staff or crozier. Stokes and Strachan translate it as 'servant of the rods'.

41. *Is úar gaeth...* see Note 42.

42. *Tabraid biad, tabraid dig...* (Source: Meyer, K. (1891) 'Fingal Ronáin', *Revue Celtique*, XIII, 368-97; Greene and O'Connor; Lehmann). Late 9th/early 10th c. Mainly seven-syllable lines. This long prosimetric, fictional text tells the story of how King Ronan's first wife, by whom he had an only son Mael Fhothartaig, died, after which he married a much younger second wife, against his son's advice. She tried to seduce the son, who went to Scotland for a while to avoid her. On his return, she persisted and when he continued to reject her, she falsely accused him and his foster-brother Congal of having her, whereupon the king had both killed (the jester who jumps up also dies and a raven picks at his entrails). The other foster-brothers killed the stepmother's family in revenge, bringing their heads to the court, whereupon she killed herself. As Ní Bhrolcháin (2009: 74-76) notes this text has generated

a lot of scholarly comment both in terms of its story (which has parallels with Phaedra) and its striking, sinewy prosody (on both aspects see Mac Gearailt, 2006-7) Charles-Edwards (1978) provides a lucid analysis of the social norms and concepts, such as honour, shame, status and the importance of solemn public utterance, which drove the actions of the various characters in such a 'pre-state society'. Since the verse falls into several sections it is difficult to translate. I have translated one of the early stanzas separately as No. 41, since it seems to me to stand on its own (the metre differs also). I am indebted here to Dennis King's fine existing translation in his online *Sengoidelc* (2013); mine differs only in three words. In line 4 of the Irish Meyer (p. 389) gives the variants of *etrom/ etrainn* (between me/us). Omitting the dialogue between Ronan and his wife, my other stanzas form the core lament for his son. Daithlinne and Doiléne are two hounds; such hounds were so important that they were sometimes regarded as servants. Uhlich (2006) comments on these stanzas in passing although his main focus is on two that I have omitted. The bare, repetitive style is powerful; I have attenuated the repetition with some variation in English, which I think is needed in translation. The penultimate line (*éo finn fota for lassair*) is problematic. Both Meyer and Lehmann think this refers to a salmon whereas Greene and O'Connor relate it to a tree. Moreover whereas Ó Cathasaigh (1985) translates the final word *lassair* as 'shining' Greene and O'Connor prefer 'blazing'. Both Thurneysen and the DIL relate the word to flames, and this does contrast with the 'cold' resting-place in my penultimate line. However, I see no reason why the tree should be burning, and think the image relates to the shape and height of a flame which some trees resemble, being broad at the bottom and narrower and pointed at the top. Dumville discusses the end of the story, after the verses I have used: see Dumville, D. (1979) 'The conclusion of Fingal Ronáin', *Studia Celtica*, 14, 71-73. Mac Cana (1997) notes that the first half of this text is in prose and the second (which I have translated) in verse. This would seem to bear out his initial, broad statement that prose was the 'natural medium for telling a story' and 'verse was the appropriate medium for lyrical expression...' (p. 102). However, as his detailed analysis of the origins, patterns and functions of prosimetric forms goes on to show, things are more complex. As regards the origins, some prose texts may have built on pre-existing poems while others had poems intercalated in them subsequently. In terms of patterns, the most common seems to be a prose text with a few poems at heightened moments, but in others the prose and verse alternate fairly evenly. The function of the verse is typically lyrical but may also be evidential, reiterative, didactic or ritualistic, and the situation is complicated by the existence in some texts of 'prosodically stylised speech' which is a kind of poetic prose, quite different from the normal register and deliberately high-flown and obscure. (Rhythmically alliterative speech was called *roscada*.) Although he acknowledges that prose is the basic language of medieval Irish stories, he concludes: 'the use of verse within prose narratives has deep roots in insular oral literature and that, given the inherent bias and selectivity of the scribal tradition, its actual range and frequency may be inadequately reflected in the written corpus.' (p. 126).

43. *Ní fhetar...* (Source: IT, Vol. 3, p.19, no. 52, variants; Greene and O'Connor). The latter translate *bán* as blonde which is no doubt right but just seems too modern to me.

44. *Arann na n'aighedh n-imdha...* (IT, Vol. 4 (1), 10-11.) For translations see Standish H. O'Grady, *Silva Gadelica: a collection of tales in Irish*, Williams and Norgate, London, 1892, p. 109; Kuno Meyer, *Ancient Irish Poetry*; Kenneth Jackson, *A Celtic Miscellany*; Lehmann. This poem comes early on in the *Acallam(h) na Senórach*, the Colloquy of the Ancients, one of the longest old Irish texts, a collection of stories which Finn's nephew Cailte (or in another version Oisin) supposedly recounts to St. Patrick several hundred years later as part of their dialogue. Present and past are skilfully interwoven in the narrative, and of course the actual audience would have had the vantage point of many centuries later than either character. Patrick asks him where the best hunting of all was for the Fianna, and Cailte describes the island of Arran in the Clyde, where they used to go each year, returning to Ireland when the cuckoo began to sing. Unlike No. 46, there is no evidence that this poem pre-dated the *Acallamh* and it forms part of the natural flow of the text. However, its pattern of cumulative,

short, descriptive phrases is similar to other early, nature poems in the Finn cycle listed by Murray (2012). I have altered the order of the descriptions to make the poem flow better in English, but the Gaelic has its own pleasures, such as the line about the fat swine: *mín a mag, méth a muca*. Lichen was used for dyes, but the word *corcra* could mean either crimson or purple. Composed in the late 12th or early 13th century, the *Acallamh* imagines a dialogue seven hundred years earlier, containing stories which go back centuries before even that. In one way it seems like the last hurrah for the heroic, pagan world (although the *Duanaire Finn* would resurrect the tradition in a later century: see No. 6). However, this idyllic little poem is not really representative: as Nagy (2005) points out the fianna lived fast and died young, and there is the sense that ultimately this ethic was going nowhere, and would in due course be overtaken by Patrick's more pacific one. Nevertheless, it is a pivotal text, juxtaposing pagan and Christian, mobile bands and settled farmers, perhaps even the ancient, historical shift from a hunter-gatherer to pastoral economy. The fianna have some affinities with the Japanese samurai, as outsiders with their own strict codes and initiations who were both feared and admired by ordinary folk. (While 'fianna' is spelled with a double 'n' in Modern Irish, one usually finds it with a single 'n' in the old texts.) On the historical and social context of the work see Dooley, A. (2004) 'The date and purpose of Acallam na Senórach', *Éigse*, XXXIV, 97-126. For an annotated translation of the entire text see Dooley and Roe (1997/2008) or the freer version by Harmon, M. (2009) *The Dialogue of the Ancients of Ireland*, Dublin: Carysfort.

45. *Dámad ór in duille donn...* (IT, Vol. 4 (1), 4; Lehmann). *Acallamh na Senórach*. See Note 44. This poem is Cailte's early response to Patrick's question as to whether Finn was a good man. Later, he is described as not only generous but just: if he had to choose between his enemy and his son in some dispute, his sense of honour would compel him to be fair. Towards the end Cailte, reflecting on his own life, says that he kept to his oath by killing only men of noble birth. The overall message is that the *fiana* had their ethic, although it would be superseded by the Christian one.

46. *Géisid cúan...* (IT, Vol. 4(1), 24-5; O'Faoláin; EIL; Lehmann). *Acallamh na Senórach*. See also Parsons, G. (2004-5) 'Acallam

Na Senórach as Prosimetrum', *Proceedings of the Harvard Celtic Colloquium*, Vol. 24/5, Harvard University Dept. of Celtic Languages and Literatures. The origins of this poem are obscure, and it seems to have become incorporated into two subsequent works: the *Acallam*, of which there are two recensions, and the *Cath Fionntrágha* (The Battle of Ventry), the latter first edited and translated by Meyer (1885: 54-7). On the former see the relevant chapters in Arbuthnot and Parsons (2012) and the entire volume edited by Doyle and Murray (2014). The strength of the *Acallam* lies in its prose tales rather than poems which often merely supplement the narrative, but this is a fine exception, with its roll-call of names, iterative lament and many allusions to cries and sounds. Parsons, having discussed several earlier, conflicting articles concludes that the poem almost certainly pre-dates the *Acallam* although she argues that it has been quite skilfully worked into the narrative, pointing to some likely adjustments: for example, whereas the stanzas have a short three-syllable first line, the final one is 7/7/7/7 incorporating a name linking the hero *Cáel* to the Finn cycle. In S1a I have translated *cúan* as 'bay' rather than harbour or haven since the description indicates quite a wide stretch of water, with breakers on both shores. The word typically means a small landing-place as in the original Irish name for Strangford Lough, *Loch Cúan*: the sea-lough of small harbours. However, *Cúan na gCaorach* in Donegal refers to the large bay of Sheephaven (one theory is that this was a mishearing of *Cúan na gCurrach*, i.e. Boathaven). The *Acallam* and *Cath* both set the poem in relation to the Battle of Ventry in which the hero Cael, supporting Finn, drowns while fighting off an invader, who also drowns. Although Ventry is sometimes called a harbour, the name is an anglicisation of *Finntrágha* or *Fionntrá* which refers to a beach, which indeed it has; there is no reference to a *cúan*. In S4 I have translated *eilit* as hind (cf Meyer's *Cath*) rather than doe since it refers here to a female red-deer rather than fallow-deer. The lamentations of the natural world which form the middle of the poem might be seen as yet another expression of the general themes of sorrow and weeping in the *Acallam* which have been explored by Mills (2013). In S5d O'Faoláin has 'a trestle under his head' rather than a cross above but the latter seems more likely although anachronistic in a pagan setting (another Christian adjustment?). In S10a, *corr* has been translated variously as 'woeful' (O'Faoláin) 'strange' (Murphy; Lehmann) and 'swelling' (Dooley and Roe, 2008). However the DIL (2012 C 484.63) gives *corrach* (derived from 1 *corr*) as rough, restless or turbulent in relation to the sea and I think it probably means this, with the –*ach* omitted because of the short three-syllable line. The sense is also consistent with *trom* (heavy) in S10b and *géis* (roaring) in S10d. Dooley and Roe (2008: 13) translate the final line as a positive ('his shield in battle screamed') which given the various manuscript variants is possible. However, I have stayed with Murphy's *nír géis* since this silence contrasts with the cries of everything else: the bravery of the shield represents that of the warrior, as O'Faoláin makes clear. The final word also forms a *dúnad*. The personal reference to 'looks' near the end might suggest that this poem was written by a woman, but such sentiments would have been a normal part of the bardic repertoire. We simply do not know.

47. *Boimm is boim...* (Meyer, K. (1897) *Zeitschrift für celtische Philologie*, 1, 456.) Original in *Leabhar Breac*, p. 176, inscribed in the margin. (See Note 24.) Gluttony is also the subject of the most famous early Irish satire, *The Vision of Mac Conglinne*, probably written in the late 11th/early 12th century, of which there exist several very readable translations. The latter is a parody of the spiritual *aisling* or vision, in a mixture of prose and verse. In one part of the poem, Ireland is imagined as composed entirely of different kinds of food and drink (butter, cheese, bacon, beef, bread, honey, beer, etc) bearing witness to the relative richness of the diet of the time. The temperate climate, fertile soil and small population all combined to create something that seems to have gone well beyond subsistence, the main threats coming from poor harvests or periodic epidemics affecting livestock.

48. *An frimm a Rí ríchid ráin...* (This poem is on one of the detached pages of the Book of Leinster (MS Franciscan A3) edited by M. O'Daly (1940) *Éigse* 2, 183-86 and subsequently translated by Greene and O'Connor.) Middle Irish version of older poem. Uncorroborated attribution to 6th c. St. Kieran who died young. It is very different from the invocatory style of the pagan plea for long life in No. 5, presenting instead a series of arguments that the writer clearly hopes will persuade

his Maker. The first word is not the familiar interrogative but derived from the verb *anad*, to wait (O'Daly has *an rim...*). I have translated *aingel finn* as 'bright angels'. *Finn* is a common and complex adjective, meaning blond, fair or handsome in a human context, right or true in a moral one, and bright or blessed in a spiritual one. As noted by Greene and O'Connor this is a problematic text: two examples will illustrate. In S1d, Mairin O'Daly has '*is sanct cech sen*' (holy is every old person) arguing that the Latin loanword *sanct* must here be an adjective. However the DIL cites only examples of it as a prefix (e.g. Saint Brigit) and I have therefore followed Greene and O'Connor's *am santach sen* (I am envious of old men). By contrast in S8d where O'Daly has '*is bec mo thorbae dond úir* (I am of little profit to the earth) Greene and O'Connor have *is bec torbai duitt ind úr* (clay is little profit to you), deleting *mo* and adding *duitt* (to you) without any basis in O'Daly's variants. Here I have gone with the older version.

49. *Batar inmuini trí toib...* (BL; MIL). Probably 8th c. Attributed to the wife of Aed mac Ainmirech who was killed in 598. I have expanded it a little so that the roll-call of names makes sense. Both Tara and Tailltu are mentioned in *The Metrical Dindshenchas*, Vol. 1, Temair V (ed. E. J. Gwynn).

50. *Tánic sam slán sóer...* (KM, 20-3). Meyer suggests 10th century. This poem has also been translated by Greene and O'Connor and Lehmann. I have primarily used Meyer's text. See also the article by Carney (1971). On the construction of these seasonal poems see Note 79. The poem is driven along by the repeated phrase *día mbí*, meaning summer... 'therefore' or 'so that'. It has intricate aural qualities e.g. *foss n-oss ro gab tess/gairid dess cass cúan*, but teeters on the edge of cliché. In the latter line I have translated *dess* (cf DIL *déess*) as indolent, but have had to lose *gairid*. The second line in the final Irish stanza (*dedlaid lim fri sín sal*) has been translated in different ways by different people; mine leans on the word *sal*, which the DIL gives variously as dirt, impurity, dross, sin, stain. In his introduction to *The Silver Branch*, Seán O'Faoláin (1938) comments on the impersonality of much of the early nature poetry, which somehow achieves its effect purely objectively: there is no romantic luxuriating in the subjective. The personal reference of *lim* (me) is thus unusual, and I have tried not to make too

much of it. Finally, back to the initial phrase *slán sóer*, literally 'healthy free', which I have paraphrased as 'well-being'. Even with our own fears, it is difficult for us now to imagine the ignorance and panic associated with strange, inexplicable diseases which would afflict the population for no apparent reason. Another poem gives a list of these including 'clouds of plagues', 'the red disease' and 'poison of the winds' (see O' Kelleher, A. (1910) 'A hymn of invocation', *Ériu*, 4, 235-240). The adjective *sóer* will be familiar to some from the Modern Irish *saoirse*, freedom (also a name). Here it does not have a political sense, but rather describes the way people could relax in this season, free from the trials and tribulations of the colder, stormier months. However Murphy (1956: 294) gives *sóer* (and *rosair/sáer/sair*) as 'noble or perfect', and Carney uniquely follows this in his translation. I suspect the poet put the two words together because they made a good opening.

51. *Brigit bé bithmaith...* (TP, Vol. 2, pp. 325-6). Date uncertain. Also quoted in part as a fine example of early Irish poetry in Douglas Hyde's bilingual *Irish Poetry*, Dublin: Gill, 1902. Short, five-syllable line. Known as Ultan's hymn, the poem is preceded by several fantastical accounts of how it came to be written. St. Brigit was the best-known female saint of the Irish church who inspired great devotion, here to the point where she is identified with the Virgin Mary. Known also as Mary of the Gaels, the fact that her feast-day coincided with that of a pagan goddess has not gone unremarked. The various forms of her name are found in many place names, including for example Kilbride, and her beautiful reed cross was adopted as the logo for Irish Television. The reference to devils in this poem and others raises the issue of the congruence of medieval and modern spirituality. Many modern readers will be able to identify in general terms with the spiritual tenor of some of these old poems, and admire, even if from a distance, the obvious piety of the writers. However, there are two aspects of such faith which may seem alien. The first is the emphasis on mortification of the flesh which took much more extreme forms in the past than it does now. The second is the belief not just in the devil, but devils: agents whose presence (like that of angels) was indubitably real to medieval Christians, as can be seen from the grotesque and striking carvings in some European cathedrals. The Arabic *jinn*, of which 'genie' is a

corruption, is an equally malign presence; the nearest modern secular equivalent is perhaps the technical 'gremlin' which originated in aviation.

52. *Daith bech buide...* (BL; Greene and O'Connor.) Date uncertain. Bees were an important part of the agricultural economy, providing both honey for sweetening and wax for candles, and there was a whole legal tract (*bechbretha*) regulating their ownership and care; see Ó Cróinín (pp. 106-7). It is difficult to translate *comol* in the last line, but it seems to me to have a strong legal sense, implying a kind of social contract or joint association, hence my 'orderly'. As noted earlier, I suspect there may have been a social subtext in some of the 'nature' poems. For example in the crane poem above, there is a definite reference to the social structure (low-born/gentleman) and there may be a message in this one about community. Bees have been seen as a social exemplar in other places in European literature (cf Mandeville, Tolstoy) and their extraordinary cohesion and discipline may have contrasted with the frequent anarchy of human society.

53. *Cú Chuimne...* (W. H. Hennessy (ed.) (1887) *Annals of Ulster*, Vol 1, Dublin: HMSO, p. 208; see also John Kelleher (1979) *Too Small for Stove Wood Too Big for Kindling*, Dublin: Dolmen, p. 10; MIL.) This eighth century monk (the 'hound of words') was a compiler of texts in the monastery of Iona and author of a Latin hymn in praise of Mary. The Annals describe him as 'a wise man' and say that this poem was sung by his nurse. Hennessy translates *caillecha* as 'hags' and while this may be an appropriate word in some poems Cú Chuimne would surely have gone after more attractive females. There is a more pious version of the poem in the *Liber Hymnorum* which is discussed in Ní Donnchadha (1994-5). She argues that *caillech* originally covered the three main categories of Christian women (married women, virgin nuns and holy widows) and that 'veiled' might sometimes refer not to nuns but to the veiling of brides at the marriage ceremony. She also suggests that the term *caillech* later extended to mean witch. There is a substantial literature on the worldly but also mysterious figure of the cailleach.

54. *Énlaith betha bríg cen táir...* (Lehmann, R. (1980) '"The calendar of the birds" and "A grave marked with Ogam": two problem poems from the *Book of Leinster*', *Études Celtiques*,

17, 197-203.) The poem is reprinted in her subsequent book (1982). From the *Martyrology of Tallaght*, originally part of the *Book of Leinster*. Probably about 830, though some suggest an earlier date, e.g. 790. This is a beautiful but obscure poem. The references in it, especially to Maelruain, suggest a connection with the reforming Céli Dé movement which Richter (2005: 98-102) thinks arose as a reaction against the growing worldliness of the church and its entanglements in local politics. The Martyrology is a calendar of saints' days, and the poem provides a parallel calendar of birds. It uses Roman terms such as calends and nones, which I have avoided because of their unfamiliarity to us now. Lehmann notes various issues in the text, but the main problems lie in stanza four, which she radically reconstructs. Like her, I can find no connection between St. Maelruain who founded the monastery of Tallaght and the Bodb/Badb which was a malevolent Celtic spirit of war and death and who sometimes appeared as a crow before or during a battle, terrifying and confusing its victims. (Lehmann refers to the Badb as 'she' presumably on the assumption that it was a manifestation of the evil Goddess Morrigan.) The phrase *ná ruc Badb (nar rug bad* in the manuscript) could mean that it did not manage to carry off Maelruain in battle, implying that the latter's peaceful Christian ethic triumphed over pagan strife. The existence of many prehistoric graves around Tallaght (the name derives from these) may have influenced the writer, or it may simply mean that Maelruain rose above local political conflicts. In the penultimate stanza, the phrase *mblíadna mbán* might be translated as 'golden age'; *bán* can have associations of purity and blessedness. (It is a complex adjective: see the reference to 'white judgements' in O' Kelleher (see Note 50). But one manuscript has *buan*, which means lasting, enduring or continuing (Thurneysen, 1975: 543) so that another translation might be 'six thousand long years'. The rising seas seem to prophesy some kind of apocalypse, like a second Flood, but presciently relevant to our own times.

55. *A Dhe tuc dam topur nder...* (Carney, J. (1939) 'A miscellany of Irish verse', *Éigse,* 1 (4), 239-48). No later than 12th century and probably much earlier. Originally from some detached pages of the *Book of Leinster*, which came to be known (because of their long-time keepers) as Franciscan; now in the possession

of the National University of Ireland. (Carney's reference to p. 40 is corrected to p. 37 on the UCD website *Thesaurus Linguae Hibernicae*.) Like some others in this collection, this little poem is more complex and composite than at first appears. Wells were important in pagan Ireland, and seem often to have had magical significance. With the arrival of Christianity, they may have been used for baptism (see chapter 3 in Bhreathnach, 2014) and some became associated with saints (cf J. M. Synge's play *The Well of the Saints*) and therefore places of pilgrimage. The poem combines these resonances with the Christian liturgical motif of tears, familiar to monks from the Latin *lacrima*. The reference to moisture and growth adds a third, natural element to the poem. The word for well (old Irish *topur*, modern *tobar*) is part of many place names, such as Ballintubber, Tipperary (*Tiobraid*), and Tobermory in Scotland.

56. *Meallach liom bheith* ... I have seen two versions of the original: Meyer, K. (1905) *Zeitschrift für celtische Philologie*, 5, 496; and O'Rahilly, T. F. (1927) *Measgra Dánta: Miscellaneous Irish Poems*, Vol. 2, Cork University Press, pp. 120-21. There is an additional stanza near the end of the former, and the spelling has been modernised in the latter. Probably 12th c. I have translated the first eight stanzas out of O'Rahilly's eleven; after that it becomes more stylized in the conventional religious way. I tried initially to reproduce the unusual 8/4/8/4 stanza, which has a lovely movement, but found that my short lines were not always as short as the Irish, so I opted for the more open form here, linked by 'so that': each stanza in the Irish begins '*go*'. There have been a number of translations, dating back to the 19th century, and the poem is well known in Ireland, having been learned by heart by some school-children. This is probably a poem about St. Columba/Columcille, often headed *Colum Cille fecit* (i.e. made it). The first word, *meallach*, is typically translated as pleasant/pleasing but this is too anodyne; the poem has a powerful sense of wish or desire, indicated by the subjunctive *bheith* in the first line and the subsequent *go bhfaicinn*... (see Stifter p. 265ff on the use of the subjunctive). It is not clear whether Columba is describing an island setting (Iona?) or imagining being back in Ireland (for the story see No. 80). Despite the 'Ulster' that has crept

into some translations, there is no specific place reference in the first line, simply *a n-ucht oiléin* (the bosom of an island, although here it means on rather than in the bosom). That said, for me the poem recalls the Donegal coast and the massive Atlantic swell, near where I grew up. The 'great sea-creatures' (*miola mára*) are probably whales or basking sharks. As will have become clear by now, the sea is an important element in many early Irish poems. This stems from the fact, of course, that Ireland is an island (with many smaller islands) but it may also reflect the relative ease of sea-travel as compared to land-travel. Thus the inhabitants of north-east Ulster would have found it easier to go across to nearby Scotland than to make their way through the various forests, bogs and marshes that lay between them and the rest of the country. The exile of Columba was a potent theme for later poets: see Herbert (2005).

57. *Úar ind adaig...* (IT, Vol. 3, 67; Greene and O'Connor). Undated. I have translated *déroil* by 'base' but I suspect the sense of 'bass' is there in the Irish also. The description of the wind as *glan* is problematic, and might equally be 'clean' or 'pure'.

58. *Do bádussa úair...* (Eoin MacNeill (1908) *Duanaire Finn*, Part 1, D. Nutt for the Irish Texts Society, London, p. 80; EIL). Probably 12th c. Five-syllable line. The poem refers to the old age of the mythical Oisin. Hair is often described as *buide*, which cannot surely be yellow: here I have gone for 'golden'. I could have used 'seduce' rather than 'impress' but felt it was too obvious. The last line of the Irish is very neat: *ní bía mar do bá* (I will not be as I was).

59. *Ro cúala...* (BL; EIL, p.90). Possibly 9th c. The poems in this selection lie largely outside the professional bardic tradition, which was embedded in the social structures of the time and performed important historical and panegyric functions. Katharine Simms' *Bardic Poetry Database* (accessible online) lists only 6 poems occurring before the mid 12th century; by the early 13th the number has jumped to 63, and the great bulk of bardic poetry comes after that, thus lying outside the parameters of this book. Bardic poetry could be highly complex in terms of prosody and Stifter (2006: 307-8) includes one exemplary poem which has a different metre, and the name of that metre, in each stanza. This neat little poem

expresses what was probably a common bardic complaint but also a general object of satire: meanness (see McLaughlin, 2008: 12-13). Its last line memorably consists of a single word: *bó* (cow) which as McLaughlin notes (pp. 23-4; p. 190) was associated with *bóaire*, meaning a commoner who herded cows. The poem implies either that the recipient was a low status commoner or a nobleman acting like one. I think the latter is more likely since a commoner would not normally be the recipient of a praise poem in the first place.

60. *In men meiles in muilenn...* (Stifter (2006, p. 174) who reproduces it from Mac Airt, S. and Mac Niocaill, G. (eds.) (1983) *The Annals of Ulster.* Dublin: Dublin Institute for Advanced Studies; see also the CELT electronic edition of the same title edited by Donnchadh Ó Corráin and Mavis Cournane. This is the second of two similar stanzas from the Annals which is a Latin/Irish history of Ulster year by year, the poem being listed as AD 650 (651 in the CELT edition). The Annals were compiled in the 15th century, but the sources may come from part of a hypothesised, lost ancient 'Chronicle of Ireland' (see Charles-Edwards, 2000, p. xix). Seven-syllable lines rhyming a/b/d; note the alliteration in the first line. The note in the 1983 edition explains that it refers to the murder of two Ulster princes by Leinstermen in a mill near Mullingar. In line 3, 'tree' means a noble family and the CELT edition inserts *genealogical* in italics before it; *forglu* literally means the pick or best part.

61. *In regsa a Ri inna rún...* (Meyer, K. (1915) *Zeitschrift für celtische Philologie*, X, 45-7.) No earlier than 10th c. There is no accompanying translation although he translated stanzas 1, 2, 8 and 9 in his *Ancient Irish Poetry*. Greene and O'Connor (pp. 151-2) limit their translation to nine stanzas on the grounds that the other 20 were added, and I have followed them. They label the poem 'The Pilgrim' but I think it may be about the practice of *peregrinatio pro Christo*, temporary or permanent self-exile as a form of piety. This was associated with St. Columbanus (d. 615) and also with the 'white martyrdom' distinguished from green or red martyrdoms in the 7th/8th c. Cambray homily (see *Thesaurus Paleohibernicus*, Vol. 2, 244-47). This poem has a regular seven-syllable line, rhyming mainly b/d, which together with its clear grammatical structure (the repeated 'whether I/without') gives it a powerful momentum,

which I have tried to capture with a basic three-stress line. In the first line, 'mystery' (*rún*) no longer has the associations in English of the Mystery Plays, and I have paraphrased instead. The 'birch-twigs' in stanza four probably refer to an uncomfortable bed rather than self-flagellation, although that was practised. In the same line Greene and O'Connor translate *búaid* as 'virtue' but the DIL states that in a religious context it can have the sense of a prize, ironic perhaps here. In the final stanza they translate *réil* as 'bright' but the word also has strong associations of purity and I have gone for 'immaculate'. 'Mil' in my stanza five refers to the legendary founding dynasty of the Irish Celts who supposedly came from Spain. This is a pivotal poem which brings together the life of the noble, the warrior ethos, piety and the surrounding sea.

62. *Fil duine...* Best, R. I. and Bergin, O. (eds.) (1929) *Lebor na Huidre: book of the dun cow*, Dublin: Royal Irish Academy, 1929. 9th or 10th century. Also included in Greene and O'Connor. A fragment of a version of the great Irish love story of Diarmuid and Grainne. See also 'The Pursuit of Diarmaid and Gráinne' in Ó Catharsaigh (2014).

63. *Aithbe damsa bés mora...* (EIL; MIL; Greene and O'Connor; Ó hAodha (2002) in Bourke (ed.) *The Field Day Anthology of Irish Writing, Vol. IV: Irish Women's Writing and Traditions*, Cork University Press, pp. 111-15.) *ca.* 800. While earlier scholars assumed this was by a man some recent ones have argued that it was written by a woman poet called Digde, hence its heading in the *Anthology*. First edited and translated by Meyer, this famous poem has been translated by many people, notwithstanding serious textual problems. Murphy thinks that seven of his 35 stanzas may be corrupt and I have further doubts about one which refers to blindness in both eyes despite a stanza which begins 'I see on my cloak the marks of age'. Omitting three other stanzas which I find problematic I have translated 24 in all. The poem is irregular, combining *rannaigecht* and *deibide* forms. Some of the many textual issues should be noted. In some manuscripts, there is a negative in the first line (*dam cen* rather than *damsa*). In stanza 1, I originally assumed that *sentu* (old age) not *mora* (sea) is the subject of the fourth line and translated: 'and although I am grief-stricken/it consumes me happily'. This takes *loan* literally as 'food' but others have

suggested that it is a metaphor for full tide, or even a variant of *lán*, meaning full, and I now think the latter is more likely. In S2d, Murphy translates *aithléini* as 'cast-off smock'. However the DIL gives the prefix *aith-* before a noun as meaning 'second, further', hence my 'change of'. The word *léini* is interesting in itself. The DIL suggests that the root *lín* may be derived from the Latin *linum*, but flax and linen predated Christianity by some centuries, and indeed one myth holds that they were introduced by a tribe that settled on the slopes of Slievenamon in Co. Tipperary. Linen was important in medieval Ireland not only as a material of everyday dress but as the cloth of surplices and shrouds, the latter supposedly including that of St. Patrick. In stanza 7, whereas Murphy and everyone else read *tocair* as an early form of *tocraid* (to seek) I originally translated it as 'abandoned child or foundling', following DIL *tacair/tocair* (e) giving 'like a freezing abandoned child/my body searches for that glorious dwelling/where it will be made welcome'. This fits *co n-aichri*, which refers elsewhere to bitter weather (*Is acher ingaith innocht* ...) which other translators have been forced to humanise (e.g. 'full of bitterness') but it leaves the line without a verb. To complicate matters further, Greene and O'Connor, using a different manuscript, have 'my body fearfully seeks its way to the house of judgement'. I have reverted to the accepted meaning of *tocair* as 'to seek' and have translated *co n-aichri* as 'desperate'. In the next line, *dochum adba dían aithgni*, I have hedged my bets on whether *dían* is an adjective qualifying *adba* (house) and meaning strong (DIL *mo les ndían*) or glorious (DIL *doss dess dian degduine*) or whether it is an adverb indicating speed, eagerness or readiness (DIL *dían garta*). Murphy leaves two syllables blank in the final line of his stanza 24 (my 20) whereas Ó hAodha has *do-rata [cró clí] fri feirg*. Some translators read this as referring to the blood and body of Christ; my speculative translation is closer to Greene and O'Connor's. Lastly, Murphy reads the lines in his stanza 25 (my 21) as separate and merely juxtaposed. However, the lines in the other quatrains are generally linked up and form a whole, so I have treated the second line as qualifying the first and leading on to the third and fourth. The poem can be read in either of two ways: first as the lament of an old woman (*sentainne*) for her (pagan) youth, only partly consoled by (Christian) religion: secondly as a poem of the archetypal, mythological *caillech* (veiled woman) reflecting on her multiple lives which are now coming to an end. For a discussion of the latter see Carey (1999) and of the wider associations of Bui see 'The Eponym of Cnogba' in Ó Cathasaigh (2014). On the subsequent influence of the *caillech* theme in Irish writing see Welch (2014). Although the prose introduction in one manuscript supports this wider interpretation, I see little in the poem itself to justify it, and suspect that the prose was added later; another problematic example of the relationship between prose preambles and poetic texts. And while Ó hAodha's encyclopedia entry for the poem does mention the mythical references, he places the accent on the human (see Koch, J.T. and Minard, A. (eds.) (2012) *The Celts: history, life and culture*. Santa Barbara: ABC-CLIO). Bitel (1996, p. 134) thinks the woman may have been a royal concubine who, lacking the formal security of marriage, has fallen on hard times. Finally, I find the quite literal reading of the poem as a lament for old age proposed by Ritari (2006; available online) the most persuasive of all. The poem also raises a more general issue. It is useful to distinguish between problems of meaning and problems of tone. It is all too easy to impose inappropriate, modern tones on such old material. Here the issue is not so much modernity as the long tradition of both personal and communal lament in Irish poetry, what might be called the *ochón ochón* (alas alas) note. While this poem clearly is a lament, it does not wallow: there is a good deal of energy, thought and criticism in it, and I have tried to bring these out as well. Although sad, it is sharp.

64. *Int én bec...* (IT, Vol. 3, 99, no. 167; BL; EIL). 10th c. The estuary here is Belfast Lough. The CELT project uses Murphy's text which has *charnbuidi* ('heaped with yellow') in the last line, rather than Carney's or Dillon's *chrannmuige* (well-wooded plain). Meyer's *Bruchstücke* also has the former, though gives the latter as a variant. This is one of the best-known of early Irish lyrics, and it is interesting to ask why. The accessibility of some of these poems has sometimes been put down to their human element: we can identify with the monk who has a pet cat, or with the scribe who sits writing in the woods. However, this little poem has no element of subjectivity, no 'I' except in

the most minimal sense of an observer, a seeing eye. But this also makes it seem wholly modern in a quite different way, that of the 20th century 'objectivist' poets who tried to excise romantic sentiment and subjectivity, and to locate the poetry entirely in the object of description, as here.

65. *It é saigte gona súain...* (Meyer, K. (1905) 'The Song of Créde, daughter of Guaire', *Ériu*, 2, 15-17; EIL; Greene and O'Connor; Lehmann). Both Meyer and Murphy omit stanza 3, as I have, on the grounds that it is incoherent. Probably early 9th c. *Debide* form. Some attribute the poem to Guaire's wife. As noted above, the preambles to poems that one sometimes encounters may have been added by a later editor and thus need to be treated with caution, since they can attempt to spin the poem in a particular way. The one here implies that Créde fell in love *after* seeing her beloved killed in battle (in AD 659) thus turning the poem into a celebration of male heroism. However this conflicts with the intimacy of the text, for example the repeated *toeb/toebthaise* (side/soft-sided). I have therefore translated *gnasa* as 'love-making' following on from *serccoí* (*serc* means love and *serc(a)id* is a lover) rather than the more anodyne 'times spent' (Murphy) 'company' (Greene and O'Connor) or 'companionship' (Lehmann). It is worth noting the unusual syntax of S1a: 'it is these, the arrows...'. In S4c, I have translated *inderb* as 'uncertainty'; the opposite *derb* means sure or steady. Others have translated it as 'instability' or 'waywardness' and in one version Lehmann has 'more free'. I think the underlying sense is perhaps the movement beyond the fixed, imposed morality of female adolescence into the less clear-cut world of the adult woman who experiences attraction, conflict and choice. In S4d others translate *théte* as 'wantonness' which is possible as Christian self-judgement, but undermines the theme of love; I have therefore gone for 'desire'. The image of a flame was sometimes used for a hero or saint but may have pagan origins (see No. 42). I follow Meyer and differ from Murphy in thinking that Cille Colman refers to a church, and the grave to Dinertach's. This is a complex and powerful poem both in terms of the expression of strength of love, the willingness to abandon the poetess's own people (*túath*) which would have been a major step in that culture, and the conflict between personal desire and conventional Christian morality.

66. *Cuilén caitt...* (*Leabhar Breac*, p. 164, bottom margin, see note 24.) Rhyming a/b, c/d. The poem is followed by a prose sentence which reads: *ata in catt geal oc dul for foendhel uain:* 'he was a fine cat but went wandering off in his own good time'. It is unusual to find a poem followed by a prose summary like this. Either the scribe, devastated by this feline betrayal, wrote both, or added his own gloss to an existing poem. In any event, it is a neat little stanza. In line 3, *míad* means honour or respect appropriate to rank, here applied to the kitten; I have tried to indicate this deference by my syntax. There are four fine poems from the *Leabhar Breac* in this collection and the scribe emerges as either an accomplished poet or good anthologist.

67. *Ro loiscit na lámasa...* (Meyer, K. (1884) *Revue Celtique*, VI, 185-6; EIL; Eoin Neeson, *Poems from the Irish*, Mercier, Cork, 1967, p. 48). Probably 12th c. Seven-syllable lines rhyming b/d. Meyer's translation differs from the later ones in several lines, and he could not understand the final stanza and left it untranslated; Murphy also notes that it is obscure, but I have followed his tentative reading here. The poem is as if spoken by Oisin, son of Finn, who was magically taken away to the land of eternal youth for several hundred years, but turned suddenly into an old man when his feet accidentally touched the ground of Ireland again. A lament for the old heroic age, but now in the mouth of a Christian. In S3c, *tláith* could mean vigorous rather than pleasant or gentle. The root word meaning sorrow or wretchedness (*trúaigh*) occurs three times in the poem, like a refrain.

68. *In acabair...* (Meyer, K. (1909) *A Primer of Irish Metrics*, Hodges Figgs, Dublin, 24; for a translation see O'Connor 1959.) The word *áth* means 'field of battle' but more specifically a ford, which if rivers were used as boundaries of territories would have been a likely place for a clash. The final phrase is striking in Irish: *a scíath ar a scáth.*

69. *Mithig techt tar mo thimna...* (van Hamel, A.G. (1917-19) 'Poems from Brussels MS. 5100-04', *Revue Celtique*, 37, 345-52; see also Poppe, E. (1999) 'Cormac's metrical testament', *Celtica*, 23, 300-11; note that his Irish text, though not his translation, has been omitted from the online pdf version. Seven-syllable line, quatrains with variable rhymes. There

are various manuscript versions of the poem, which Poppe suggests is 12th century. It appears to be the last testament of a king-bishop of Cashel in Munster, who had to go to fight a battle in the neighbouring province of Leinster. Such persons had both spiritual and temporal roles, so it is quite possible that he was engaged in such a conflict. As is evident in some of the early poems in this collection, the provinces of Ireland were important demarcations in its early history. The poem's construction is by no means hasty or last minute and it is likely that it was actually composed well after Cormac's death. The list of people and places, and the order in which they occur, raise the possibility that its subtextual purpose may have been to affirm certain ecclesiastical power structures in Munster; Poppe explains the various references and explores this angle. For all that, it is a fine and curiously moving poem, with the writer's obvious distress at relinquishing his cherished objects somehow increasing one's sympathy for him, while betraying a certain worldliness. As noted above, the poem is usually referred to as Cormac's 'testament' but Ward (1973) argues that *tiomna* has the sense of a mandatory will rather than a dying statement. While the end of the poem is the latter, the bulk of it is clearly a will, and I have therefore preferred that term. Nor, *pace* Poppe, do I think there is any 'discussion' in the first line: Cormac is setting out his decisions. Compared to van Hamel's, Poppe's edition twice changes the order of stanzas and makes some 20 other textual amendments. I have largely followed his reading, although I translate *bennach* literally as 'blessed' rather than 'decorated' although the latter sense is implied by what follows. 'Laver' is the Latin for a washing-basin. A typically insoluble translation problem occurs in stanza 4, with *cá húaisle arra*? A modern equivalent might be 'what better form of payment' but nobility was an important feature of and concept in the society then, so I have retained it, even though it sounds a bit odd now. My translation of the poem is relatively prosaic, because I have tried to capture something of the repetitive, stately, almost liturgical rhythm of the Irish, which seems to me unique among the poems I have translated.

70. *Ni mhair glún*...(Meyer, K. (1892) *Irisleabhar na Gaedhilge/ The Gaelic Journal* Vol IV, No 40, p. 114.) From *Leabhar Breac*.

Undated. Seven-syllable lines, rhyming a/c/d. A conventional sentiment, but powerfully expressed.

71. *Íomarrat do ndebaingil...* (Fr. Patrick Walsh (1911) *Irish Ecclesiastical Record*, XXIX, 528-9; EIL). 7/5/7/5 stanza rhyming b/d. Attributed to St. Patrick, 5th c. although probably much later. Walsh reproduces an earlier text of Meyer's, but gives his own translation which reads well: *may thy holy angels attend/ our sleep, our rest/our bed with beauty.* Murphy notes that in line 6 of the original (and my translation) the usual possessive pronoun *dúin* (our) has been changed to *dún*, to rhyme with *run* (with a *fada* in Walsh but without in Murphy) meaning 'mysterious' and both Meyer and he translate simply as 'in our sleep'. However, the word *dún* also means fort or stronghold and while I don't think early Irish poetry involved much word play, the coincidence would not have been missed and I have taken advantage. I have found it difficult to get the tone, as distinct from the sense, right in this poem. I have tried to reflect the simplicity and directness of early Irish Christianity in some of the language, but it was not simplistic and the danger is that we project backwards a kind of lost innocence. The belief system was already imbued with the complex doctrine of the Trinity, and subsequent Celtic scholarship would become extensive, as the religious glosses and commentaries in TP show. See the relevant chapters in Ó Cróinín.

72. *Is acher in gáith in-nocht...* (TP, Vol. 2, 290; MIL). This quatrain captures the fear felt by the inhabitants of coastal areas in particular of the Viking raids which began in 795 and continued on and off for the next two centuries, sometimes using the rivers to reach well inland. The Vikings also established trading settlements which were the origins of a number of Irish towns and cities. Their power diminished after their defeat by Brian Boru at Clontarf in 1014, though it was not quite the climactic event I was given to understand at school, and they remained a presence in Ireland, gradually integrating with the locals. This poem was probably written about 840 or 850, so the timing makes sense. Various possible locations have been suggested, one of which is an island monastery in Strangford Lough in Co. Down. The name itself is Viking, meaning narrow fjord, alluding to the narrow entrance to what opens out into quite a wide and long, island-studded lough. The poem appears as a gloss in the St. Gall Priscian: a single long line across the top

margin of the page. The initial letters IS are in capitals. There seems to be a mid-line dot after what is now transcribed as the second line of the quatrain, and at the end two full stops and an upward short stroke, perhaps indicating conclusion (unlike the downward comma at the end of the first line of *Dom-farcai*). The word *minn* has been omitted and then added above the line with what looks like a colon marking the insertion point. The dots after *innocht* and *minn* in TP are not there. There are two textual issues. In the third line of the original, *mora minn* is sometimes translated as 'the Irish sea'. I see no grounds for this. *Minn* is probably a variant of *menn*, meaning clear (cf TP 'clear sea') though I suspect has the sense of 'open sea'; hence I have translated it as 'ocean'. The DIL translates *menn* as 'clear' in the sense of evident or visible, not calm. It also points out that the translation of *mora minn*, which is not capitalized in the original, as Irish Sea, does not appear in Edmund Hogan's *Onomasticon Goedelicum* and may thus be more modern. The other problem comes in the final line. The scribe has written what seems to me to be ó *a*. TP and others including Ahlqvist below have interpreted this as the preposition úa, though the NUI Galway edition transcribes it as *o,* superscript *u, a*. It is possible that the glossator corrected himself or changed his mind as he wrote. Whatever the reading, the preposition precedes the noun *lothlind*. This spelling is unusual though not unique and the DIL states that it means any Viking base in the British Isles, rather than necessarily Scandinavia. Ahlqvist disputes this, arguing that it means something like 'mud pool' perhaps referring to a base near Dublin (*Dubhlinn* means 'black pool') and (following Ford's reasoning on the positioning of glosses) relates to a line of Latin in the text which refers to 'poisonous slime'. Although the poem is on the same page, there is some distance between it in the top margin and the Latin which is 17 lines down the first column. In any case the connection seems tenuous and the poem itself suggests the open sea rather than some coastal raid. I suspect instead that the variability of old Irish spelling probably accounts for Lothlind; in any case a scribe who omitted one word and left another unclear might not always be accurate. See Ahlqvist (2005).

73. *Is scíth mo chrob...* (Meyer, K. (1921) *Zeitschrift für celtische Philologie*, 13, 8; EIL). Probably 11th or 12th century. Seven-

syllable line rhyming b/d. A number of translations exist, including an internet video of Seamus Heaney reading one. Along with St. Patrick and St. Brigit, St. Columba/Columcille was one of the three great saints of the early Irish church and indeed his fame seems to have surpassed them at times. He was particularly associated with writing (his exile was popularly supposed to stem from a bloody copyright dispute) and so it is wholly appropriate that this poem about manuscripts is associated with, but not by, him; he died in 597. It is one of a large number of poems ascribed to him but almost certainly written much later to venerate him. The second line *ní dígainn mo glés géroll* is problematic. The DIL gives *dígainn* as 'copious, abundant' so I take *ní dígainn* to be the opposite, following on from the sense of the opening line. In contrast, Meyer translates the second line as 'my sharp quill is not steady', Murphy as 'my great sharp point is not thick', and Lehmann as 'stout', none of which seem right. *Glés* actually means equipment or writing instrument, and this obliqueness seems to me part of the rather wry tone of the poem: the reference to the *selba ségann* (my 'eminent people') at the end reminds me of the modern art collector. I hope they did it for the right reasons, but the weariness of the scribe certainly comes through. Although *dub* commonly meant ink, the DIL gives 'pigment' for *dúbhach* with *dúbhach na peann* specifically referring to pen-ink. I have translated the wider associations of *gan scor* (never unyoked, unharnessed) in the penultimate line of the original rather than merely the sense of unceasing.

74. *Fada la nech mar atú...* (Meyer, K. (1892) 'Anecdota from Irish MSS', *Irisleabhar na Gaedhilge/The Gaelic Journal*, Vol. 4, No. 40, p. 115.) Seven-syllable lines rhyming a/b and c/d. Undated.

75. *A Chrínóc cubaid do cheól...* (Meyer, K. (1908) 'Mitteilungen aus irischen Handschriften', *Zeitschrift für celtische Philologie*, 6 (2), 266.) See also MIL; Greene and O'Connor; Lehmann. Both Meyer and Lehmann include a 12th possible stanza. Attributed to the 11th century cleric/poet Mael Ísu Ua Brolcháin. It was originally thought that this poem referred to a woman called Crinoc who, following the practice of the times, tested the virtue of clerics by chastely sleeping with them, but Carney pointed out that this is probably a conceit for the cleric's cherished psalter, lost and found again near the end of his life. There are various uncertainties in translation. In the first

line, *cubaid* could mean either a poetic/musical measure or by extension 'fitting' or 'proper' i.e. it is fitting that I sing of you. On balance, I have opted for the former. S2b: Carney suggests that *níata* connotes a female warrior who instructed young nobles; a further conceit. I have paraphrased it as 'strong' but others have used 'valiant'. S2c: *daltán clíabglan caem nád cam: clíabglan* is a compound word meaning 'clean cradle': *nád cam* might mean 'not bent' (as the old poet now physically is) or not crooked i.e. innocent. S3d: I have translated *geilt* here as 'rapt' in a positive sense, but it can mean wild, frenzied or crazy, as in the Sweeney cycle. S4cd: *is ferr rográd dod gaeis géir/ar comrád réid risin ríg.* The UCD edition has *'na* instead of *ar*. Although all the above sources have seen fit to capitalize *Ríg* i.e. God, leading to some contorted translations, there is no capital in the manuscript (see ISOS: UCD collection, Franciscan MS A9, p. 20). I think the contrast is therefore between the internalized dialogue with the acute 'mind' of the psalter and the bland conversation with an earthly king. Frank O'Connor's translation in Crotty (2012: 13) also conveys this sense. S9d: I have treated *ní gó* as a cheville.

76. *Is aire charaim Doire...* (Stokes, W. (1887) 'Betha Choluim Chille', *Three Middle-Irish Homilies*, privately printed, p. 108; EIL; for a variant see the second stanza in O'Rahilly, T.F. (1927) *Measgra Dánta*, No. 46, p. 126, Cork University Press.) From *Leabhar Breac*. Usually associated with St. Columba although Murphy gives a 12th c date. Widely known and translated. This little poem so precisely strikes that Celtic note of sensory spirituality that it defies translation. The first problem is *gloine*, which Stokes translates as purity and Murphy as brightness; the first on its own is too simply spiritual, the second too merely sensuous. (I have noted before that *glan* is a powerful but complex word; see its various meanings in the DIL.) The other problem is *finn*, which we have encountered from Cú Chulainn (see Note 4) onwards, and for which translators in the past used the old English 'fair' but which often means white. In line 2 also *réide* basically means level or smooth. However, it cannot be this physical sense here, since Derry is hilly, and so the figurative sense of tranquil or even pleasant seems appropriate. In addition *lomlán* means something like 'chock full'; it is a very concrete word to use of such ethereal beings.

77. *Bennocht ocus édrochta...* (Best, R.I. (1910) *Ériu* 4, p. 120.) Undated. Seven-syllable line, irregular rhyme. The first two lines of the third stanza are problematic: *foroan Trínóid togaidhi/ré cách, iar cách do ellacht.* The DIL gives *togaidhi* as 'chosen' or 'excellent' and Best uses the first; my 'above all' is intended to capture both senses. He tentatively translates *do ellacht* as 'has been united' and 'universal'. I am unsure whether it relates to the *Trínóid* or *cách,* but have tried to catch some of the unitary emphasis with 'three-in-one'; I wonder if *cách* refers to people but hope my biblical 'all things' is inclusive of them.

78. *Bóeth da cach duine...* (Meyer, K. (1892) *Irisleabhar na Gaedhilge/The Gaelic Journal,* Vol. IV, No 40, p. 115. Originally in the margins of the *Leabhar Breac* (see note 24). The full first line means 'what fools are people in this world' but I have gone for a shortened version to balance my short last line. Meyer could not make sense of the last word in the poem, *achaer,* and left it untranslated, but it is simply *ach aer.* I love this little poem which seems to me to bring together the formal piety and love of the natural world which characterised the society. One of the striking and appealing features of that culture is the way the divine and the natural seem to have been congruent rather than at odds with each other. As noted earlier, such congruence can be underpinned by various theologies or ideas. One is the neo-Platonic view that the world is an emanation, as distinct from creation, of God, that there is an element of the divine in everything and everyone, if only one can see it, a notion which for example is expressed in some Sufi poetry. There is also the kind of vague pantheism one finds in Wordsworth, which comes close to believing that the world – nature – is God. The old Irish view strikes me as different from either of these. Nature is loved because it, like man, is God's creation, a manifestation of His Goodness which surrounds us and continually reminds us of that fact. The result is that the perception and description of nature in early Irish poetry remain wholly naturalistic rather than symbolic, while at the same time forming part of the grand scheme of things.

79. *Cétemain cain cucht...* (The earliest printing I have come across is in Meyer, K. (ed.) (1881-3) 'Macgnimartha Finn inn so sis', *Revue Celtique,* 5, pp. 201-2, no. 20, without line breaks; KM, 8-11; O'Rahilly, T.F. (1927) *Measgra Dánta,* Vol. 1, p. 59; EIL). 9th c. See Murphy, G. (1955) 'Finn's poems on May-day'

Ériu, 17, 86-99; see also Carney's criticism of his text in Carney, J. (1970) 'Notes on early Irish verse', *Éigse* XIII (4), 291-312. I have selected the first seven stanzas of this poem which then runs into textual problems and also becomes repetitive; and I have reversed stanzas 6 and 7. There are variations between the Irish texts; I have mainly followed Murphy. Tymoczko (1983) analyses the metrical and prosodic construction of this and other 'seasonal' poems, pointing out that they work cumulatively, capturing not a single experience but the typical, essential features of the season, and aggregating these to form a composite picture. In this, they are quite different from many modern 'lived' nature poems, and can seem rather bitty in translation, piling one thing on top of another. (Tymoczko calls them 'staccato' and compares them to a film montage.) However, their formal unity binds them together: like many old Irish poems, this one employs strong alliteration as well as rhyme and assonance. The VSO (verb-subject-object) syntax gives a powerful initial impetus to many lines, and Tymoczko notes the relative absence of definite articles and the use of the generalised *cach* (each). The poem supposedly forms part of the Finn cycle and the prose preamble states that the hero composed it to demonstrate his prowess as a poet, which status would hopefully bring him various practical and tactical advantages. Tymoczko thus treats it as a visionary poem, exemplifying the supernatural powers of the seer rather than ordinary sight (see also Nagy, 1981). However, as with other prose-poetry links (see Mac Cana, 1997) it is not certain that the poem did originally form part of the Finn saga, and it strikes me as stylized rather than visionary, a fine example of a particular genre of nature poetry. In any case, Dooley and Roe (2008: xiv) argue that the poetic or visionary reputation of Finn stems from the confusion or conflation of two quite different figures, the warrior Finn mac Cumaill and the Leinster Finn File (Finn the poet). However, what could be more appealing than the idea of a poetic warrior? I have retained 'lacerated' since although it may seem rather modern, it directly translates the Irish, capturing the connotations of battle and wounding; again I suspect there are human and social allusions in what seems on the face of it to be a 'nature' poem. Finally, old Irish poetry had, like all poetries, its clichés: horses are always swift, lakes brimming, peace perfect, as here.

80. *Fil suil nglais...* (Contained in the *Amra Choluim Chille* in the *Lebor na hUidre*, p.11; EIL; MIL). 11th c. This famous quatrain Is said to have been composed by St Columba as he left the shores of Ireland to go into exile in 563. His original name was Columcille, meaning dove of the church, but unfortunately the peaceful connotations of this were not borne out, and (as noted above) legend has it that after a dispute over a manuscript with another saint which led to a bloody battle, he was forced to leave Ireland and went to Scotland where he founded the monastery of Iona. There is a Glen Columcille in Co. Donegal and the original Irish name of Derry/ Londonderry was *daire Choluim Chille*, the oakwood of Columcille. The colour *glais* is yet again a problem, but although I love Murphy's 'blue' here (the landscape reflected in the eye?) I think sadness is the dominant sense. Carney's 'grey' is dull in English, so I have gone in a different direction. As noted earlier in this collection, colours are a problem in early Irish poetry. The topic is explored in a fascinating article by Siewers (2005). This includes a diagram (p. 44) which relates colours to points of the compass: north is black, south white etc. However, the associations are complicated by a partly overlapping relationship with the chromatography of martyrdom. Alas, none of this makes the translator's job any easier. For a longer poem in which this quatrain is the second stanza see Eoin Neeson, *Poems from the Irish*, Mercier, Cork, 1967, pp. 140-42. Although that poem is rather disjointed it does contain some fine lines, including the following stanza in praise of his native land: 'melodious her clerics, melodious her birds/ gentle her youths, wise her old men/famous her nobles and her leaders/ famous her women as loving wives'. Late in his life, President Douglas Hyde published a *Songs of Columcille* in 1942, evincing his deep love of this poetry. Symmetrically, my book began with a poem of arrival and ends now with one of departure. The theme of leaving has resonated with Irish emigrants for many decades, and moreover this little verse is almost accessible to modern Irish-speakers because of the familiar words *suil* (eye) *firu* (men) and *mna* (women). Indeed 'the backward look' became an established phrase after Frank O'Connor's survey of Irish literature with that title. Whether, after the dramatic economic growth and then collapse of the

last quarter-century, it still has the same force, is an open question.

81. *Ní discéoil duae Néill...* An extract from near the beginning of the *Amra Choluim Chille* attributed to the poet Dallán Forgaill, who was a friend of the saint. Dated 598. (Note the self-deprecating 'unlettered' reference in the middle; others have translated this as 'fool'.). Charles-Edwards (2000: 289) thinks the poem may have been commissioned by Aed Mac Ainmirech, a relation of Columba and king of Tara. For the text and translation see Whitley Stokes (1899) *Revue Celtique*, 20, 31ff, 132ff, 248ff, 400ff. I have also consulted the recent translation and modern Irish version by P. L. Henry (*Amra Choluim Chille*, Ultach/Gaelic Arts Agency, 2006) which differs slightly from that by him included in *An Leabhar Mór* (online). The poem is irregular but with some repeated words and phrases at the beginnings of lines, paralleled in the translation. Quite a few lines have no verb, making the verse particularly dense; Thurneysen (1975: 326) notes that the verb is sometimes omitted in poetic descriptions. The text is complicated by the interpolation of subsequent 11th century glosses which attempt to explain what was even then an archaic poem. My translation is quite rhetorical since I think that in this case the original demands it. There is no simple English equivalent for the stylish Irish *ní discéoil* (not without news) at the beginning. Charles-Edwards (2000: 441) notes that this is the first reference to the O'Neill dynasty. While the classic Irish hillfort had disappeared by about 800BC, it still seems an apt word for *duae* here. I have unpacked the following lines *ní uchtat óenmaige/mór mairg, mór deilm/dífhulaing ris ré asneid* to try to give them their full resonance. I have omitted the obscure reference to the fairy poet Nera in the middle of the poem. 'Tay' refers to the river in Scotland and Columba's work in converting the Picts. *Huile bith ba háe hé*: this is a striking but difficult line. (The DIL gives the variants of *ba hai he, ba he aai, ba haoi ae*.) The syntax order is SVO but this was allowable with the copula. However, there are two pronouns, both of which are in the rarer emphatic form (Stifter, 2006: 171). Literally it reads 'the whole world it was his he' and other versions I have seen have understood it as 'the whole world was his' (although the 11th century gloss suggests that

the final word might mean 'alas'). This is possible as Dallán's poetic, hyperbolic statement of Columba's influence, though it borders on blasphemy: to the pious, the world is surely God's. I think that risk can be avoided by treating *bith* here as referring to the people of the world. In the final line *chéis* is translated by tuning-key, rather than (possibly) small harp. Such keys were and still are used to tighten or loosen the strings by turning the pegs. The poem ends this book on the note of lament into which Irish poetry so often conventionally falls, but here is a genuinely moving eulogy (*amra*).

V. Originals

Since I have not attempted to reproduce the prosody of the Irish in my translations, for the reasons spelled out at the beginning of these notes, I have appended the originals of seven poems here so that readers can see what they actually look like. In most cases, I have gone back to an early edition to show how the poems first appeared, and it will be seen that what are now sometimes called quatrains were originally set out in a different form. Since the first great flowering of Celtic studies between about 1880 and 1920, an effloresence that was truly international, and which is now largely available online, the scholarly enterprise has continued, in terms of reconciling different manuscript versions, clearing up obscurities and normalising or modernising spelling. (Unfortunately, this usually means adding modern punctuation, which I think is inappropriate.) However there remain considerable textual difficulties and uncertainties in many cases and these obviously feed through into translations. We cannot always be sure, and the texts should sometimes be regarded as simply the best guess.

Even readers who do not know Irish should get some sense from these texts of the form and prosody (alliteration, rhythm, rhyme and assonance) of the poems, and their stylistic sophistication. Often it is their extraordinary compactness which is striking: a feature which is very difficult to reproduce. I think it is rare for translations from any language to be as tight as the originals, but the syntax makes Irish particularly concise. Over and above that, I sense that economy of expression was highly prized among these poets, and it is no accident that when comparisons have been made, they have sometimes been with Chinese or Japanese poetry, rather than neighbouring European models.

1

Ticfa táilcend tar muir meircenn :
a bratt tollcend, a chrand cromchend :
a mías inairthuir a tigi :
fris [g]erat a múinter huili,
    'Amen, amen'.

Source: Stokes (1887) *The Tripartite Life of Patrick*, p. 34. Carney's updated
version has different spellings, line-breaks and inserts the missing line as
'*canfaid míchrábud*' ('intoning impiety') after *cromchend*. He also points
out that 'amen' is close to an Irish word meaning 'thus' and translates 'be it
thus'. The poem starts with a verb *ticfa* (will come) which gives it an initial
impetus; I have transposed the poem into the dramatic present. In this
poem the patterning is provided by sheer repetition, not only of *cend/cenn*
(head) but the pronoun *a* (his). In other ways it is irregular. I suspect this
shows its very early oral origins: it would have been easy to memorise and
repeat.

9

Atomriug indiu

niurt Dé   do'm luamaracht
cumachta Dé   do'm chumgabail
ciall Dé   do'mm imthús
rosc Dé   do'm reimcise
cluas Dé   do'm éstecht
briathar Dé   do'm erlabrai
lám Dé   do'mm imdegail
intech Dé   do'm remthechtas
sciath Dé   do'm dítin
sochraite Dé   do'mm anucul

ar intledaib demna
ar aslaigthib dualche
ar irnechtaib aicnid
ar cech nduine mi-dústhrastar dam

i céin ocus i no-ocus
i n-uathed ocus hi sochaide

Source: Bernard and Atkinson (eds) (1898) *The Irish Liber Hymnorum*, Vol. 1. London: Henry Bradshaw Society, p. 134. While the content of the poem known as St. Patrick's breastplate is clearly Christian, the much older pagan form of it becomes clear from this section of the text. Although many lines have six or seven syllables the metrics are irregular and any rhymes seem fortuitous. Even alliteration is scant: the whole impact relies on insistent repetition, of *Dé do'm* and then *ar* and *i*. This makes it closer to incantation than verse. There are similar incantatory poems in the *Lebor Gabála Érenn: the book of the invasions or taking of Ireland* (see the edition and translation by R. A. Stewart Macalister) which are attributed to Amergin, supposedly a poet of the Milesians (Celts?) and thus sometimes regarded as the first Irish poet; although the LGE is an 11th century creation and we cannot be sure of the age or provenance of such poems. More generally, this text opens up the question of the relationship between oral and written tradition. Before the advent of Latin, the transmission of poetry would have been entirely by ear, and one can hear how memorable this text (or its possible precursors) must have been. Once in written form, early Irish poetry developed highly refined prosodies, as is evident from the other originals reproduced here.

Messe ocus Pangur Bán   cechtar nathar fria saindan
bíth a menmasam fri seilgg   mu menma céin im saincheirdd.
Caraimse fos ferr cach clú   oc mu lebran leir ingnu
ni foirmtech frimm Pangur Bán   caraid cesin a maccdán.
Orubiam scél cen scís   innar tegdais ar noendís
taithiunn dichrichide clius   ni fristarddam arnáthius.
Gnáth huaraib ar gressaib gal   glenaid luch inna línsam
os mé dufait im lin chéin   dliged ndoraid cu ndronchéill.
Fuachaidsem fri frega fál   a rosc anglése comlán
fuachimm chein fri fegi fis   mu rosc reil cesu imdis.
Faelidsem cu ndene dul   hinglen luch inna gerchrub
hi tucu cheist ndoraid ndil   os me chene am faelid...

Source: Stokes and Strachan (1903) *Thesaurus Paleohibernicus*, Vol. 2, p. 293. 12 of the 16 lines. Rhyme scheme: *deibide*. The poem is now typically printed in quatrains, as in EIL, p.2. The name of the cat is Pangur Bán, and the poem is often known by that. Irish metrics are complex and the early scholars, perhaps influenced by the study of Latin and Greek, devoted a lot of attention to them. (There is a useful chapter at the end of Stifter, and Murphy analyses the metres in each of the poems in his book). The essential point for the general reader is that almost all the poems in this book are syllabic. Whereas the English iambic pentameter consists of five, two-syllable feet with a stress on the second syllable (di-da di-da di-da...) the Irish line is based on a straight syllabus count with no regular stresses. Thus the first line here can be counted simply: *mess-e oc-us pang-ur ban*. This is the common seven-syllable *deibide* line/couplet, and carries on throughout the poem. There are quite complex rules for counting particular sounds, and the lack of regular stress does not preclude the natural syntactic emphases of the language. Flower (1947: 24-5) reproduced this pattern in his well-known translation: 'I and Pangur Ban my cat/'tis a like task we are at'. O'Connor (1959:14-15) thought this ignored the slower pace of the original and translated instead: 'Each of us pursues his trade/I and Pangur my comrade'. In contrast, I have unstitched the original pattern altogether, primarily to avoid a jingle and to try to get across a more conversational, intimate tone.

17

*Domfarcai / fál fomchain loid luin lúad nad cel . huas mo lebran ind
linach fomchain trirech immanén ..., / fidbaide*

*Fomchain coi minn medair mass limbrot glass de dindgnaib doss.
debrath nomchoimmdiu coim/ cainscribaim foroide r(oss)*
                              /a

This shows as nearly as possible how this poem actually appears as
marginalia in the St. Gall Priscian manuscript, held by the Stiftsbibliothek,
and now available at e-codices.unifr.ch/de/csg//0904/203/medium

The first line appears on the bottom margin of p. 203, the second likewise
on p. 204. The top and bottom margins are wider than the vertical ones,
although there are numerous explanatory glosses in the latter, usually
at the sides of the page but occasionally in the space between the two
columns of text.

Each long line begins with a capital. The dots halfway through are actually
mid-line rather than base-line. Note the two periods and comma at the end
of the first line/ page. Although there are three length marks (*fada*), the
others that we would expect are left out; this was quite common in texts
of the time (mid-9th century). Double 'm's are indicated by a diacritical
mark above the letter which cannot be reproduced here. Note the two
emendations, of *fidbaide* in the first line, and *coima* in the second. The
final word of the second line cannot be read clearly, having been obscured
by page-turning finger-marks. Rhyme scheme: *rannaigecht.*

22

Scél lém dúib
  dordaid dam
snigid gaim
  ro faith sam.

gáeth ard uar
  ísel grian
gair a rrith
  ruthach rían.

roruad rath
  ro cleth cruth.
ro gab gnath
  giugrand guth.

ro gab uacht
  ete én
aigre ré
  e mo scél.

Source: Best and Bergin (eds) (1929) *Lebor na hUidre*, p. 30. I have corrected what was a transcribing error in the last line; for a fully corrected version with normalised spelling, see EIL. The extraordinary conciseness of this beautiful little poem about the onset of winter is clear from its layout. This compactness is achieved partly by the very short three-syllable line; I cannot think of any such lines in English poetry ('ding dong bell' is actually in stressed metre). However it is also due to the way words are simply juxtaposed: *gáeth ard uar* means lexically 'wind high cold' and *ísel grian* 'low sun'. Of all the translators of early Irish poetry, I think Flann O'Brien/ Brian O'Nolan best captures this kind of linguistic terseness, though almost to the point of parody: see his version in Montague (1974, p. 79). The poet skilfully uses the repetition of *ro* to carry the poem towards its conclusion: the first *(ro)ruad* means 'very', the subsequent ones are past tense forms. Note that the poem ends with the same word as it begins with, an example of *dúnad*, closure. *Scél* is quite difficult to translate: as well as 'news' it has the sense of a tale or story; which is why I have chosen it as my title.

25

Fuitt co bráth!
is mó in donenn ar cách
is ob cach etrice án
[ocus] is loch lan cach áth

[Is] méit muir mór cech loch lonn
is drong cech cuiri gúr gann
mét taul scéith banna dond linn
mét moltchrocann find cech slamm

Méit cuithi cach lattrach léig
coirthe cach réid, caill cach móin
na helta ní [co]sta dín
snechta finn fir doroich tóin

Ro-iad réod róta gribb
íar ngléo glicc im Choirthi Cuilt
congab donenn dar cach leth
co ná abair nech acht fuit!

Source: Meyer (1903) *Four Old-Irish Songs of Summer and Winter*. To avoid confusion, I have replaced the horizontal length-marks in Meyer's text with the usual *fada*/acute accent in this and the next poem. The brackets give a small indication of the many textual problems facing early scholars of old Irish, and much work has subsequently been done on reconciling different variants and normalising spelling, which varied widely. This is an example of a very well constructed poem. After the short, dramatic opening line, it has a seven-syllable line with b/d rhymes and some additional rhyme/assonance. The rules for what counted as rhyme were complex and differed somewhat from our own. The repetition of the word *mét/méit* (the size of) builds the emphasis well, as does the repeated *cach/cech* (each, every). The specific place reference near the end somehow pins the poem down and the conclusion comes round nicely again to the beginning; again a case of *dúnad* (closure).

Céttemain cáin ré
rosáir cucht and
canait luin láid láin
día mbeith lái gái gann

Gairid cái crúaid den
is fochen sam sáir
suidid síne serb
imme cerb caill cráib

Cerbaid sam súaill sruth
saigid graig lúath linn
lethaid folt fota fráich
forbrid canach fann finn

Fúabair boscell sidin scéill
imrid réid rían rith
ré 'na cuirither sál súan
tuigither bláth bith

Berait beich – bec a nert
bert bond bochta bláith
berid búar slaib fri slíab
feraid seng saidbir sáith...

Source: Meyer (1903) *Four Old-Irish Songs of Summer and Winter*. First five stanzas. This poem employs a five-syllable line and the rhyme scheme is a form of *rannaigecht*. The driving force of the verbs (ending in –id or -it) at the beginning of lines is again apparent. Although the poem most obviously rhymes lines b and d in each stanza, there are also examples of a kind of aural chaining from one stanza to the next: *gaí* in the last line of stanza 1 is picked up by *gairid* in the first line of stanza 2, *cerb* in 2 by *cerbaid* in 3, *for-beir* in 3 by *fúapair* in 4. (For the formal and rather complex rules governing such chaining see Stifter, 2006, p. 306). However, the most striking prosodic feature is the alliteration, sometimes of every word in the line, although again there were strict rules governing what counted as alliteration in Irish, and not everything that we think would, did. Meyer uses dashes to separate off *bec* a *nert* where Murphy (EIL) has parentheses. Whatever the typography, these kinds of additions or asides are not uncommon in old Irish poetry. Murphy also amends the text at the beginning.

VI. Glossary

As noted earlier, medieval Irish poetry is often a poetry of naming, of key figures, mythical or historical, and significant places. The following list is limited to the most important of these.

Adze: a curved medieval cutting instrument, used here as a rude description of St. Patrick's curved tonsure.

Arran: the Scottish island in the Clyde estuary where the Fiana used to go for rest and relaxation for part of the year.

Badh/Bodh (pronounced *Bav*): a mythical crow whose appearance signalled battle and carnage.

Beare: a peninsula and island in Co. Cork.

Boss: the centre or hub of a shield, which often protrudes.

Brigit: Ireland's most famous female saint, from Leinster, venerated on a par with St. Patrick and St. Columba. Variously spelled Brigit, Brigid or Brid.

Cliodna: located somewhere on the south coast which experiences the full force of the Atlantic swell.

Connaught, Leinster, Munster, Ulster: the provinces were important entities even in early times, although often referred to as 'fifths': Meath, the site of the high king at Tara, was sometimes counted separately, and Munster sometimes divided into two. The sub-division into counties came much later with the Normans who arrived in the 12th century.

Croagh Patrick: a mountain in the west of Ireland, a place of Christian pilgrimage in more recent times. Cruachu, which occurs elsewhere, probably refers to the royal seat of Connaught, in Co. Roscommon. The word generally means a stack or hill and occurs in various parts of Ireland, including the Bluestack Mountains in Co. Donegal.

Cormac: a semi-historical High King of Ireland.

Cu Chuimne: an Irish monk (d. 747) associated with the monastery founded by St. Columba/Columcille on the island of Iona off the west coast of Scotland. His name means 'the hound of memory'.

Cu Chulainn: a famous Ulster warrior hero; here *cú* refers to a guard hound that he killed as a boy, after which he swore to become the guardian of the province.

Cuilt: a place on Slieve Gullion in Co. Armagh, where there are prehistoric remains.

Currach: a rowing boat covered with animal hide, still sometimes used on the west coast.

Feidelm: a woman seer from Connaught.

Feimen: a plain near Cashel in Co. Tipperary, the seat of the kings of Munster.

Fintan: a mythical Irish poet who supposedly dated from the time of Noah and lived for many centuries, seeing and chronicling the various invasions and settlements of Ireland.

Finn: the leader of the Fianna, the most famous of the mythical Irish warrior bands. These bands, which had some historical basis, were associated with various parts of the country and were a law unto themselves, both feared and admired by the settled population. When not fighting, they enjoyed hunting and feasting.

Gae bolga: a magical harpoon-like spear.

Gobban: a builder of holy buildings such as churches and monasteries; possibly mythical, possibly historical.

King: a common epithet for God. The word was familiar, since there were several levels of king, ranging from local 'kings' (i.e. chieftains) through provincial kings to the high king, who was supposed to have ultimate authority but whose power in practice was often limited or contested.

Liadain: a female poet who fell in love with Curithir, who supposedly wrote this poem, which is part of a longer joint lament.

May-day: the important pagan festival of Beltaine.

Mil: father of the mythological sons who settled Ireland; notionally the first Celts.

Morna: a clan from the north and west of Ireland which attacked the south-east.

Moy: here a river in Co. Mayo.

Naoise (pronounced *Neeshe*): the young warrior who was seduced by Deirdre and who was pursued to his death by the older king who wanted her for himself

Oisin (pronounced *Usheen* and anglicized as Ossian): a mythical figure, son of Finn. His name means 'young deer'.

Oratory: a small prayer-site or chapel, typically in a remote place and associated with hermits or small groups of monks who lived, temporarily or permanently, outside the main monasteries.

Tailltu: a hill near Tara which was the site of royal ceremonies.

Temair: the old name for Tara, the seat of the high kings of Ireland in Co. Meath.

Thirties/thirty-hundreds: by legend and quasi-historical fact, Ireland was originally divided into areas that could raise 3,000 fighting men; each of which comprised a number of smaller settlements or *baile*, here translated as 'townlands'.

Pronunciation

Because of the phonetic differences between the two languages it is impossible to transcribe old Irish into modern English precisely. Where an English guess is likely to be reasonably close to the original I have left fairly well alone, listing only those words which are likely to throw the reader completely. Old Irish pronunciation is much too complex to be summarised here; for a detailed account see Stifter (2006: 15-24) and for comparisons of some transcriptions see Jackson (1971: 325-343) or Dooley and Roe (2008: xxxiv-xxxvii). Also, some sounds changed over the time-span of this book. The following rough guidance can however be given:

The stress normally falls on the first syllable.
'Ch' is like 'kh', 'ch' or even a breathy 'h' depending on changes over time.
'Dh' is like the soft 'th' in the English 'think'.
'Th' is like the hard 'th' in the English 'this'.
'M' often becomes a nasalised 'v'.
The short 'a' is pronounced as in 'hat'; the long 'a' is transcribed 'aw'.
The short 'i' is pronounced as in 'hit'; the long 'i' is transcribed 'ee'.
The short 'o' is pronounced as in 'hot'; the long 'o' is transcribed 'oh'.
The short 'u' is pronounced as in 'hull'; the long 'u' is transcribed as 'oo'.
Final vowels are sounded but are short.

Any transcription system short of the IPA (International Phonetic Alphabet, which employs over 150 symbols) is bound to be somewhat subjective. Also, old Irish was rather variable in its spelling and also accents, which I have typically added here. The length mark (fada) could apply not just to a vowel but to a diphthong. The letter 'h' in modern orthography often replaces the traditional dot over the letter.

4   Cú Chulainn   *coo khullen*; Muirthemne   *muirthevne*; Feidelm   *Fedhelm* (or possibly *Fedhlem*)

6   Túaidhe *tooidhe*; Clíodhna *clyodhna*; Dún da Bheann *doon da van*; Feardhomhain *ferdhovin*; Feirceart *ferciert*; Umha *uva*;

Uaithne *ooithne*; Finnumha *finnuva*; Alloidh *allidh*; Faoláin *fwaylawn*; Follomhain *follevin*; Criomhall *cruvall*; Áodh/Aedh (variant spellings) *eydh* as in '(l)ithe' the *ey* later becoming *ao* in 'they'; Oilill *ulyil*; Tadhg *tayg*; Breasail *bresil*; Sgíath Breac *sgiath breck* (modern Irish, *brack*); Aonghus *enghus*; Leagán *leyawn*; Lúachair *luakher*; Raígne *rayneh*; Aillbhe *alveh*; Óg *ohg*; Iolann *yolann*; Geimhnám *givnawm*; Uamidh *ooamidh*; Uisneach *ishnach*; Caoínche *keenkheh*.

7   Fothad Canainne *fothad cananye*

8   Aillil *alyil*; Crúachan *cruakhan*; Temair *tevir*

12 Oisin *osheen*

14 Caoilte *keeltye*

16 Loeguire *leyehre* (though some suggest a more gutteral *leghere*)

18 Croagh *croah*

23 Bruidge *brudhye*; Áed *eydh*; Ailill *alyil*; Cuilíne *coolyinye*

25 Mael Fábaill *meyl fawvil*

28 Naoise *neeshe*; Arddán *ordawn*; Aindle *anlye*

29 Emain *evin*; Uislui *ushlu*

31 Líadain *leeadan*

42 Mael Fothartaig *meyl fothartay*

43 Etan *eytan*

46 Rinn dá bhárc *reen daw vawrk*; Drum Sílenn *drum sheelan*; Tulachléis *tulachlesh*; Crimthain *crivthen*

49 Áed mac Ainmirech *eydh* (see above) *mac animrech*

53 Cú Chuimne *coo khivneh*

54 Badh *bav*

61 Míl *meel*

63 Feimen *feven*

65 Roigne *roinye*; Gúaire *gwaireh*; Irlúachair *irluakhir*; Aidne *eynye*

68 Áed *eydh* (see above)

69 Ailbe *elveh*; Mo chuta *mo khooteh*; Senán *shenawn*; Súir *shoor*

VII. Bibliography

N.B. This bibliography lists the main sources; additional sources on specific poems are given in the Textual Notes.

Ahlqvist, A. (2005) 'Is acher in gaith ... úa Lothlind', in: J. Nagy and L. Jones (eds) op. cit., 19-27.

Arbuthnot, S. J. and Parsons, G. (eds) (2011) *The Gaelic Finn Tradition*. Dublin: Four Courts.

Ball, M. and Müller, N. (eds) (2010) *The Celtic Languages* (2nd edn.). London: Routledge.

Bernard, J. H. and Atkinson, R. (eds) (1898) *The Irish Liber Hymnorum*. London: Henry Bradshaw Society.

Bhreathnach, E. (2014) *Ireland in the Medieval World, AD400-1000*. Dublin: Four Courts.

Bitel, L. (1996) *Land of Women: tales of sex and gender from early Ireland*. Ithaca, N.Y.: Cornell University Press.

Borsje, J. (2007) *The 'terror of the night' and the Morrígain: shifting faces of the supernatural* (Proceedings of the Seventh Symposium of the Societas Celtologica Nordica). Uppsala: Acta Universitatis Upsaliensis, 71-98.

Bourke, A. (ed.) (2005) *The Field Day Anthology of Irish Writing, Vols IV, V: Irish women's writing and tradition*. Cork: Cork University Press.

Breatnach, L. (2006) 'Satire and praise and the early Irish poet', *Ériu*, 56, 63-84.

Brown, T. (ed.) (1996) *Celticism*. Amsterdam: Rodopi.

Buttimer, C. (1994-5) 'Longes Mac nUislenn reconsidered', *Éigse*, XXVIII, 1-41.

Carey, J. (1983) 'Notes on the Irish war-goddesses', *Éigse*, XIX (2), 263-75.

Carey. J. (1997) 'The three things required of a poet', *Ériu*, 48, 41-58.

Carey, J. (1999) 'Transmutation and immortality in the lament of the old woman of Beare', *Celtica*, 23, 30-37.

Carey, J. (2000) *King of Mysteries: early Irish religious writings*. Dublin: Four Courts.

Carey, J. (2004) 'The encounter at the ford: warriors, women and water', *Éigse*, XXXIV, 10-24.

Carey, J. (2005) *Lebor Gabála* and the legendary history of Ireland, in: H. Fulton (ed.) op. cit., 32-48.

Carney, J. (1950) "Suibhne Geilt" and "The Children of Lir", *Éigse*, VI (2), 83-110.

Carney, J. (1970) 'Notes on early Irish verse', *Éigse*, XIII (4), 291-312.

Carney, J. (1971) 'Three old Irish accentual poems', *Ériu*, 22, 23-80.

Carney, J. (1983) 'The dating of early Irish verse texts', *Éigse*, XIX (2), 177-216.

Carney, J. (1985) *Medieval Irish Lyrics and the Irish Bardic Poet*. Dublin: Dolmen.

Carnie, A., Harley, H. and Dooley, S. (eds) (2005) *Verb First: on the syntax of verb-initial languages*. Amsterdam: John Benjamin.

Charles-Edwards, T. M. (1978) 'Honour and status in some Irish and Welsh prose tales', *Ériu*, 29, 123-41.

Charles-Edwards, T. M. (2000) *Early Christian Ireland*. Cambridge: Cambridge University Press.

Clancy, T. O. (1991) *Saint and Fool: the image and function of Cummine Fota and Comgán Mac Da Cherda in early Irish literature*. Ph.D thesis, University of Edinburgh, online archive.

Clancy, T. O. (2005) Court, king and justice in the Ulster cycle, in: Fulton, op. cit., 163-82.

Clancy, T. O. (2014) Early Gaelic nature poetry revisited, in: G. Henley and P. Russell (eds) *Rhetoric and Reality in Medieval Celtic Literature: studies in honour of Daniel P. Melia* (CSANA Yearbook 11-12). Hamilton: Colgate University Press, 8-19.

Clemens, L. and Polinsky, M. (2014) *Verb-Initial Word Orders (Primarily in Austronesian and Mayan Languages)*. To appear in the *Blackwell Companion to Syntax*, 2nd edition. scholar. harvard. edu, updated 2014, online.

Corkery, D. (1924) *The Hidden Ireland*. Dublin: Gill.

Crotty, P. (ed.) (2012) *The Penguin Book of Irish Poetry*. London: Penguin.

Deane, S. (ed.) (1991) *The Field Day Anthology of Irish Writing, Vols I-III*. London: Faber and Faber.

Dillon, M. (1994) *Early Irish Literature*. Dublin: Four Courts (reprinted).

Dinneen, P. (1927, reprinted 1965) *Foclóir Gaedhilge agus Béarla: an Irish-English dictionary*. Dublin: Irish Texts Society. Reprinted with additions 1934.

Dooley, A. and Roe, H. (1997, paperback 2008) *Tales of the Elders of Ireland*. Oxford: Oxford University Press.

Doyle, A. and Murray, K. (eds) (2014) *In Dialogue with the Agallamh: essays in honour of Seán Ó Coileáin*. Dublin: Four Courts Press.

Egeler, M. (2008) 'Death, wings and divine devouring: possible Mediterranean affinities of Irish battlefield demons and Norse Valkyries', *Studia Celtica Fennica*, V, 5-25.

Eska, J. (2010) The Emergence of the Celtic Languages, in: M. Ball and N. Müller (eds) op. cit., pp. 22-27.

Fife, J. (2010) Typological Aspects of the Celtic Languages, in: M. Ball and N. Müller (eds) op. cit., pp. 3-21.

Flower, R. (1947) *The Irish Tradition*. London: Constable.

Ford, P. (1999) Blackbirds, Cuckoos and Infixed pronouns: another context for early Irish nature poetry, in: R. Black et al (eds) *Celtic Connections*, Vol 1. East Linton: Tuckwell Press, 162-70.

Fulton, H. (ed.) (2005) *Medieval Celtic Literature and Society*. Dublin: Four Courts.

Gell-Mann, M. and Ruhlen, M. (2011) 'The origin and evolution of word order', *Proceedings of the National Academy of Sciences* (PNAS), 108(42), online.

Gensler, O. (2006) Hamito-Semitic Hypothesis, in: J. Koch (ed.) *Celtic Culture: a historical encyclopaedia: Vol 1*. Santa Barbara: ABC-CLIO, 890.

Greene, D. (1973) 'Synthetic and analytic: a reconsideration', *Ériu*, 24, 121-33.

Greene, D. and O'Connor, F. (1967, reissued 1990) *A Golden Treasury of Irish Poetry: A.D.600 to 1200*. Dingle: Brandon.

Henry, P. L. (ed.) (2006) *Amra Choluim Chille*. Colmcille/Ultach Trust.

Herbert, M. (2005) Becoming an Exile: Columb Cille in Middle-Irish Poetry, in: J. Nagy and L. Jones (eds), op. cit., 131-140.

Hewitt, S. (2014) *The Question of a Hamito-Semitic Substratum in Insular Celtic and Celtic from the West*, academia.edu (online).

Hickey, R. (2002) 'Internal and external forces again: changes in word order in Old English and Old Irish', *Language Sciences*, 24, 261-283.

Hogan, J. (1928/9) 'The Tricha Cét and Related Land-Measures', *Proceedings of the Royal Irish Academy*, 38, 148-235.

Hollo, K. (2005) Laments and lamenting in early medieval Ireland, in Fulton, op. cit., 83- 94.

Hull, V. (1949) *Longes mac n-Uislenn: the exile of the sons of Uisliu*. New York: Modern Language Association of America.

Isaac, G. (2007) Celtic and Afro-Asiatic, in: H. Tristram (ed.) op. cit., 25-80.

Jackson, K. (1953) 'A further note on Suibhne Geilt and Merlin', *Éigse*, VII (2), 112-16.

Jackson, K. (1971) *A Celtic Miscellany*. London: Penguin.

Kelleher, A. (1910) 'A hymn of invocation', *Ériu*, 4, 235-40.

Kinsella, T. (1969). *The Tain*. Oxford: Oxford University Press/Dolmen.

Koch, J. T. (2014) *On the Debate over the Classification of the Language of the South-Western Inscriptions, also known as Tartessian*. academia.edu, online (revised version).

Koch, J. T. and Minard, A. (eds) (2012) *The Celts: history, life and culture*. Santa Barbara: ABC-CLIO.

Larson, H. (2005) The veiled poet: Liadain and Cuirithir and the role of the woman-poet, in: J. Nagy and L. Jones (eds) *Heroic Poets and Poetic Heroes: a festschrift for Patrick K. Ford* (CSANA Yearbook 3-4). Dublin: Four Courts, 263-68.

Lehmann, R. (1982) *Early Irish Verse*. Austin: University of Texas.

Mac Cana, P. (1988) 'The poet as spouse of his patron', *Ériu*, 39, 79-85.

Mac Cana, P. (1997) Prosimetrum in insular Celtic literature, in: J. Harris and K. Reichl (eds) *Prosimetrum: crosscultural perspectives on narrative in prose and verse*. Cambridge: Cambridge University Press, 99-130.

Mac Cana, P. (2004) 'Praise poetry in Ireland before the Normans', *Ériu*, 54, 11-40.

McCarthy, D. (2003) 'On the shape of the insular tonsure', *Celtica*, 24, 140-67.

McCone, K. (2008) *The Celtic Question: modern constructs and ancient realities*. Dublin: Dublin Institute for Advanced Studies.

MacCotter, P. (2008) *Medieval Ireland: territorial, political and economic divisions*. Dublin: Four Courts.

MacEoin, G. (1993) 'Irish', in: M. Ball (ed.) *The Celtic Languages*. London: Routledge.

MacEoin, G. (2007) What language was spoken in Ireland before Irish? in: H. Tristram (ed.) op. cit., 113-125.

Mac Gearailt, U. (2006-7) 'The making of Fingal Rónáin', *Studia Hibernica*, 34, 63-84.

McLaughlin, R. (2008) *Early Irish Satire*. Dublin: Dublin Institute for Advanced Studies.

MacNeill, E. (1923) 'Ancient Irish Law: the Law of Status and Franchise', *Proceedings of the Royal Irish Academy*, 36C.

MacNiocaill, G. (1968-71) 'A propos du vocabulaire social irlandais du bas moyen age', *Études Celtiques*, 12, 512-546.

Mallory, J. (2013) *The Origins of the Irish*. London: Thames and Hudson.

Melia, D. (2005) On the form and function of the 'Old-Irish verse' in the Thesaurus Paleohibernicus, in: J. Nagy and L. Jones (eds) op. cit., pp. 283-90.

Meyer, K. (1885) Cath Finntrága, *Anecdota Oxoniensis*: Medieval and Modern Series Vol.1 – Part 4. Oxford: at the Clarendon Press.

Meyer, K. (1903) *Four Old-Irish Songs of Summer and Winter*. London: David Nutt.

Meyer, K. (1913) *Ancient Irish Poetry*. London: Constable.

Meyer, K. (1919) *Bruchstücke der älteren Lyrik Irlands*. Berlin: De Gruyter.

Montague, J. (ed.) (1974) *The Faber Book of Irish Verse*. London: Faber.

Murphy, G. (ed.) (1933) *Duanaire Finn: the book of the Lays of Fionn*. London: Irish Texts Society.

Murphy, G. (1939) 'Notes on aisling poetry', *Éigse*, I, 40-50.

Murphy, G. (1955) 'Finn's poems on May-day', *Ériu*, 17, 86-99.

Murphy, G. (1956) *Early Irish Lyrics*. Oxford: Oxford University Press. Since reissued by Four Courts Press, Dublin.

Murray, K. (2012) Interpreting the evidence: problems with dating the early *fianaigecht* corpus, in: S. J. Arbuthnot and G. Parsons, op. cit., 31-49.

Nagy, J. F. (1981) 'Liminality and knowledge in Irish tradition', *Studia Celtica*, 16, 135-43.

Nagy, J. F. (1988) 'Oral life and literary death in medieval Irish tradition', *Oral Tradition*, 3(3), 368-80.

Nagy, J. F. (1997) *Conversing with Angels and Ancients: literary myths of medieval Ireland*. Ithaca, N.Y.: Cornell University Press.

Nagy, J. F. (2005) Life in the fast lane: the *Acallam na Senórach*, in: Fulton, op. cit., 117-131.

Nagy, J. F. and Jones, L. (eds) (2005) *Heroic Poets and Poetic Heroes in Celtic Tradition: a Festschrift for Patrick K. Ford* (CSANA Yearbook 3-4). Dublin: Four Courts.

Ní Bhrolcháin, M. (2009) *An Introduction to Early Irish Literature*. Dublin: Four Courts.

Ní Donnchadha, N. (1994-5) 'Caillech and other terms for veiled women in medieval Irish texts', *Éigse*, XXVIII, 71-96.

Ó Cathasaigh, T. (1977-78) 'The semantics of 'Sid'', *Éigse*, XVII (2), 137-55. Reprinted in Ó Cathasaigh (2014).

Ó Cathasaigh, T. (1985) 'The rhetoric of Fingal Rónáin', *Celtica*, 17: 123-44. Reprinted in Ó Cathasaigh (2014).

Ó Cathasaigh, T. (2014) *Coire Sois: the cauldron of knowledge* (ed. Matthieu Boyd). Notre Dame, Ind.: University of Notre Dame Press.

Ó Concheanainn, T. (1973) 'The scribe of the Leabhar Breac', *Ériu*, 24, 64-79.

O'Connor, F. (1959) *Kings Lords and Commons*. New York: Knopf.

Ó Corráin, D. (1989) Early Irish hermit poetry? in: D. Ó Corráin, L. Breatnach and K. McKone (eds) *Sages, Saints and Storytellers*. Maynooth: NUI., pp. 251-267.

Ó Cróinín, D. (1995) *Early Medieval Ireland 400-1200*. Harlow: Longman.

O' Faoláin, S. (1938) *The Silver Branch*. London: Jonathan Cape.

O' Grady, S. (1892) *Silva Gadelica: a collection of tales in Irish*. London: Williams and Norgate.

O' Keeffe, J.G. (1931, reprinted 1952) *Buile Shuibhne*. Dublin: Dublin Institute for Advanced Studies.

Ó Lochlainn, C. (1943) 'Poets on the battle of Clontarf (part 2)', *Éigse*, IV(1), 33-47.

Ó Murchadha, D. (ed.) (2009) *Lige Guill: the grave of Goll*. London: Irish Texts Society.

Ó Rathile, T.O. (ed.) (1926) *Danta Gradha: an anthology of Irish love poetry (A.D. 1350-1750)*. (2nd edn.). Dublin and Cork: Cork University Press.

Ó Tuama, S. and Kinsella, T. (1981) *An Duanaire 1600-1900: poems of the dispossessed*. Dublin: Dolmen.

Poppe, E. (1999) 'Cormac's metrical testament', *Celtica*, 23, 300-11.

Richter, M. (2005) *Medieval Ireland: the enduring tradition* (2nd edn.). Dublin: Gill and Macmillan.

Ritari, K. (2006) 'Images of ageing in the early Irish poem *Caillech Bérri*', *Studia Celtica Fennica*, III, 57-70.

Schoepperle. G. (1919) 'The washer of the ford', *Journal of English and German Philology*, 18(1), 60-66.

Sheehan, S. and Dooley, A. (eds) (2013) *Constructing Gender in Medieval Ireland*. London: Palgrave Macmillan.

Siewers, A. (2005) 'The bluest-greyest-greenest eye: colours of martyrdom and colours of the winds as iconographic landscape', *Cambrian Medieval Celtic Studies*, 50, 31-66.

Sims-Williams, P. (1996) 'The invention of Celtic nature poetry' in: T. Brown (ed.) op.cit.

Squires, G. (2010) Eight lines of Coffey, in: B. Keatinge and A. Woods (eds) *Other Edens*. Dublin: Irish Academic Press, 38-46.

Stacey, R.C. (2005) Law and literature in medieval Ireland and Wales, in: Fulton, op. cit., 65-82.

Stifter, D. (2006) *Sengoídelc: old Irish for beginners*. Syracuse: Syracuse University Press.

Stifter, D. (2010) Early Irish, in: M. Ball and N. Müller (eds), op cit., pp. 55-115.

Stokes, W. (ed.) (1887) *The Tripartite Life of Patrick.* London: HMSO.

Stokes, W. and Strachan, J. (eds) (1903) *Thesaurus Paleohibernicus: Vol 2.* Cambridge: Cambridge University Press.

Thurneysen, R. (2003, first published 1946) *A Grammar of Old Irish: revised and enlarged edition* (trans. D. A. Binchy and Osborn Bergin). Dublin: Dublin Institute for Advanced Studies.

Toner, G. (2004) 'Baile: settlement and landholding in medieval Ireland', *Éigse*, 34, 25-43.

Toner, G. (2009) 'Messe ocus Pangur Ban: structure and cosmology', *Cambrian Medieval Celtic Studies*, 57, 1-22.

Tristram, H. (ed.) (2007) *The Celtic Language in Contact.* Potsdam University Press, ebook.

Tymoczko, M. (1983) 'Cétamon: vision in early Irish seasonal poetry', *Eire-Ireland*, 18(4), 17-39.

Uhlich, J. (2006) 'Some textual problems in Rónán's lament 1: two quatrains concerning Echaid's daughter (Fingal Rónáin Lines 180-7)', *Ériu*, 56, 13-62.

Ward, A. (1973) ' "Will" and " testament" in Irish', *Ériu*, 24, 183-86.

Watkins, C. (1973) 'River in Celtic and Indo-European', *Ériu*, 24, 80-9.

Welch, R. A. (2014) *The Cold of May Day Monday: an approach to Irish literary history.* Oxford: Oxford University Press.

Windisch, E. and Stokes, W. (1891-7) *Irische Texte mit Wörterbuch.* Leipzig: Hirzel.

Wooding, J. (2009) 'Reapproaching the pagan Celtic past – anti-nativism, asterisk reality, and the late antiquity paradigm', *Studia Celtica Fennica*, VI, 51-74.

Young, A. (1975) *Dánta Grádha: love poems from the Irish (A.D. 1350-1750).* London: Menard Press.

VIII. Acknowledgements

I would like to begin by remembering my mother who sprinkled some Irish on me. I must also acknowledge my profound debt to those scholars from various countries on whose painstaking work over many decades this book has drawn.

Various individuals and institutions have helped me with the preparation of this publication, and I would like particularly to thank the following:

Cormac Anderson, Max-Planck Institute for the Science of Human History, Jena; Bibliothèque Nationale, Paris; Jacqueline Borsje, University of Amsterdam; Jimmy Cummins; Fergal Gaynor, Boole Library, University College Cork; Hull City Library; Trevor Joyce; John Kearns, Editor, *Translation Ireland*; Máire Nic Mhaoláin; Mary Squires; and Augustus Young (James Hogan).

Versions of some of these poems have already appeared in *Jacket2* and a number have been read at the Soundeye Poetry Festival in Cork.

The responsibility for it all remains mine alone.

IX. About the Author

Geoffrey Squires (b. 1942) is originally from Co. Donegal and was educated at Portora Royal School, Enniskillen. After reading English at Cambridge and a spell on the Aran Islands he lived and worked in a number of countries including Iran, France and the US and then settled in England. He is now retired and living in Yorkshire.

Summer, a long poem for three voices, was broadcast by the BBC in 1971. His first two books of poetry, *Drowned Stones* (1975) and *Landscapes and Silences* (1996) were published by New Writers Press, Dublin. *XXI Poems* was published by Menard Press, London, in 1980. *A Long Poem in Three Sections* was published by *Irish University Review* in 1983 and several short poems in *The Hip Flask* anthology, Blackstaff Press, Belfast, 2000. His work has been collected in *Untitled and other poems* (2004) and *Abstract Lyrics and other poems* (2012) both published by Wild Honey Press, Bray. Three of his books have been translated and published in French as *Sans Titre* (2013), *Paysages et Silences* (2014) and *Pierres Noyées* (2015) by Editions Unes, Nice.

His comprehensive translation of the 14th century Persian poet *Hafez: translations and interpretations of the ghazals* was published by Miami University Press in 2014 and awarded the Lois Roth translation prize of the American Institute of Iranian Studies which groups all the universities that teach Persian in the US. He has given readings in Ireland, the UK, the US, France and Italy and is a regular contributor to the Soundeye Poetry Festival in Cork.

CPSIA information can be obtained at www.ICGtesting.com
Printed in the USA
BVOW04s0213171115

427435BV00001B/9/P